THE STORY BEHIND A STATUE

WILLIAM PERRY

THE TIPTON SLASHER

CHAMPION BARE KNUCKLE FIGHTER OF ALL ENGLAND

1819 - 1880

Perry Beauchamp

First published April 2011 by Perry Beauchamp Publications, 23 St. Michael's Grove, Dudley, DY2 7SE.

A CIP record of this book is available from the British Library.

ISBN 978-0-9568950-0-4
(Hardback)

ISBN 978-0-9568950-1-1
(Paperback)

Printed in England by Orphans Press Ltd, Arrow Close, Enterprise Park, Leominster, Herefordshire, HR6 0LD.

THE STORY
BEHIND A STATUE

This book is dedicated to Christine for reasons only she knows.

Know that evil is weak for it is born of cowardice. Courage is eternal for it is born of love and love never dies.

FOREWORD

I was waiting on the corner of the road outside the pub, I knew Perry was near. I was downwind. The whiff of Teddy Gray's herbals[1] wafted towards me. "I need a favour" he announced. Well I always got the first round so it wasn't that. "I'd like you to write the Foreword to me book". "Honoured," I thought. Little did I realise the task that was to befall me.

Well before you get too involved in the history and fights of Bill Perry, it might help to get a feel for the Victorian Black Country of which "The Tipton Slasher" was truly a legend. From my own research and conversations in pubs (mainly the latter) I will try to take you to that time.

London had "The Ripper". The Slasher sounds worse but got his name from the way he rained down his fists in sharp sweeping blows. He was a prize fighter, a skilled pugilist and bare knuckle boxing champion. He was a legendary character who earned the respect and admiration of all Tiptonians who revere the traditions of the past. His hammer fists were as famous as the Tipton "hommers" working away at the forge.

What was going on in the 1850s? We had the Crimean War; Divorce; the Indian Mutiny; VCs; Charles Dickens; Edward Elgar and bare-knuckle boxing.

Much went unrecorded at the time unless the Government wanted it banned then there would be legislation. The songs and poems of boatmen, miners, nail-makers, weavers etc. have been passed down and it is from here that we get much of what went on.

Sport was a cruel and bloody business. The language of the time was brutal. *Boxiana* is riddled with fancy slang: "Ogles" were blackened, "peepers" plunged into darkness, "tripe-shops" received "staggerers", "ivories" were cracked, "domino boxes" shattered, and "claret" flowed in a steady stream.

Bull baiting had bulls chained to a stake and run at by dogs trying to pin it down by the nose. A century before there was baiting of badgers,

---

1 Edward Grays of Dudley was founded in 1826 by John Gray, as he thought it would be a good way to earn a living buying and selling sweets, at the time he travelled the Black Country by horse and cart

bears, horses, lions, apes and even men (usually a hardened collier); anything that was worthy of a bet.

Wakes and fairs had horse racing and the traditional boxer's booth.

Ales, beers and stingo (a strong old ale) were consumed by all ages as the water could kill.

Fireball was a variation on village street football and was played to celebrate victories in battle with a hemp football, bound, tar soaked and lit then kicked around.

Sun Wheels were wooden cartwheels covered with hemp and tar, lit and rolled down hills to ward off witches and evil spirits.

Street fighting had young men from one street pitching into those from another that sometimes lasted weeks.

Travellers sold salt, sand, fly papers, soap, broom and water cress; rag and bone dealers hawked themselves around.

Stories of devils, imps, and fairies making knocking noises down the mines abound.

"Heaving" the lifting by men of a woman and vice versa for reward went on at Easter-time.

Singing, dancing and drinking was popular on Saturdays - pay day! Good to see we still retain some traditions.

In 1832 cholera struck in Tipton. With no NHS and little money for doctors you were as likely to be treated by a wise woman with a magic cure as you were a witch. Because of the lack of sunlight blocked out by the industrial smog of the Black Country young William Perry was weakened and deformed by rickets.

Netherton nail-makers and Kidderminster weavers went on strike for fair pay.

Edinburgh and London had the "Body-Snatchers". In the Black Country we had the "Diggum Uppers". Corpses were sold to medical schools. Granite slabs were placed on graves as a deterrent. It didn't always work as you will discover as you read on.

So what do we know about Perry Beauchamp? I first met him when he was at Burnt Tree Primary School. It was not long after when we went to Tipton Grammar that he lost interest in our system of education. Those that taught misunderstood him. They had different ideals; teachers from another place in a money starved area. But folk from Tipton have true values. Perry is a real Black Country "mon". He has spent half of his life drawing together and sorting out the history, the gossip, the rumour and the lies surrounding his hero. Form your own view as to whether he has achieved his aim of telling the true tale of the Tipton Slasher. It is not without controversy and is a bit like the Slasher - it pulls no punches. That's not entirely accurate if you believe he threw one of his fights but you'll read about that later too.

Perry reckons he probably only has four real friends. I'm just proud to be one of them. As his Grandad used to say,"It's better to have a few true mates than a lot of fake ones."

This book is tempered with the steel of authenticity and where Perry has struggled to find facts because little written record is to hand, his opinion is unquestionable.

As someone old enough to remember Round Oak Steelworks (now called "Merry Hill") I just had to share this with you this description from 1868:

"The Black Country reveals itself only at night. As the sun descends in the west it hangs the horizon with curtains of its own crimsoning. Its red twilight softens first into gold, then into pearl, and melts out of the evening sky; then comes the afterglow of the region of fire and smoke. Then up springs the aurora borealis of the Black Country – the swaling light of a hundred furnaces and forges roaring all through the night. It runs up and down the horizon like summer lightening, crimsoning the edges of the clouds, and the patches of sky between. This light is the halo around the brow of swart and patient labour – that knows no rest while wealth is dreaming in its sleep."

Walks in the Black Country - Elihu Burritt

Mike Stevens (litigator of some years with Millichips solicitors West Bromwich)

"It's in my Blood" by Chris Williams

A friend of mine, Stuart, who runs a publishing firm, happened to mention to me that a couple of guys were writing a book about Bill Perry – The Tipton Slasher. I asked straight away if I could have a copy of the book and Stuart produced the manuscript, which I duly read. For anyone like me, with a boxing background, and being a Brummie with links to the Black Country, this book is a must.

From the age of about 4 years the main topic of conversation in our household between my elder brother, my Dad and myself, was boxing.

Dad had been a very good amateur boxer in his teens, boxing out of the well-known city centre gym, at Kyrle Hall. He also boxed behind closed doors in the 1930s at picture houses and pubs in the Ladywood area on a Sunday morning. I believe this was illegal, but it went on. He would also fight in boxing booths; when the favourite came to town if you could last three rounds you would win a fiver. He also had a reputation as a street fighter, which earned him the nickname of "The Bullet". You would want him on your side if trouble broke out.

All this talk inspired me and I too boxed as a schoolboy, but sadly not in my dad's league.

In 1949 I listened to my first live fight on the wireless. It was from Madison Square Garden, between Jersey Joe Walcott and Ezard Charles. Dad would come home from the pub, have a bit of supper, get to bed and set the alarm for 2 am. All the fights seemed to start at that time. Then he would wake us kids up and we would come down stairs and listen in awe to the fight.

Up to 1966, when I left home, I never missed a single heavyweight title fight in all that time. So keen was I on boxing that with my first week's wages in 1959 I purchased "The Ring" magazine and for the next ten years or so had every copy that was printed. These times, which were hard and tough, shaped my life. These values I still treasure today.

Introduction By Perry Beauchamp

Now, in the later days of my life, before I leave this Earth, I have decided to put together an historical record of the late Tipton Slasher. Books have been written, one of which is Tom Langley's - a Bible to the Tipton Slasher, but none includes the story behind the Statue and Grave restoration through appeals since his death.

This book is a collection of newspaper cuttings collected over many years - a childhood scrapbook. Four Sovereigns they found in his grave, "So he day die a pauper then?" These words were overheard during a conversation between a group of Tipton men in the Old Bush, Tipton, and inspired me to write and record the history of a great man.

Who were the Digger Upperer's of Tipton? This book will try to tell the story of how a group of dedicated followers instigated his removal from Kate's Bonk back to Coronation Gardens, Tipton.

Many things have been said or written about Old Tipton, some are true, some are myth, some are folklore or some wishful thinking. Despite intensive research many such like stories try to portray an accurate insight into a part of history which shaped The Black Country. It is only when I leave this world, swapping this Boxing Ring for the next one in the sky and meeting the Slasher & discovering the truth, the real story of his life then I can compare his words to my book. A pity I cannot pass it on, or can I? Before you start to get into the book there are certain things that will be of interest to you and which will start a journey into the Legend of Ode Tipton and The Slasher's world of boxing, the rewards, the deceit and the friendship these gladiators of the Black Country formed amongst their ranks.

1. Tipton's Coat of Arms

9

Thanks to:

Mike Stevens

This book has been in the making for many years and has finally come to fruition with the help of one of my true mates. His enthusiasm has been second to none and I know that without his help it would still be in the top drawer where it would have lain for ever and a day. In my darkest days, and there have been a few, the thought of my problems are put into the shade when I think of his. I hope that our friendship will remain for years to come.

Gary Lynch

A true friend indeed.

Dave Pettitt

As solid a mate as the bricks he lays.

All at the WestBrom

And In memory of Frank Allen and Geoff Bennet

(Once more into the breech my friends)

And to the so-called mate

Friends never need repaying and talk is cheap

Part 1

Tribute to "The Tipton Slasher"

Another great hero has quit the scene of his exploits in the person of Mr William Perry, once known as the "Tipton Slasher". Into the merits and demerits of prize-fighting we do not propose to enter. It had its good aspect possibly: it certainly had its bad side. But the "Tipton Slasher" was one of those pugilists who did little to bring his occupation or profession into disrepute. It is on record that he fought hard but humanely, that his honesty was undoubted, and that though he eventually succumbed to the superior strength or science, or both, of Tom Sayers, he was a skilful and gallant opponent. Following upon the heels of such renowned fighters as Randall, Hudson, Belasco, Martin, Cribb, and Spring, he yet belonged to the class which considered that a rare and straight forward fight was a creditable and satisfactory performance. He and his friends at any rate held the knife and the revolver in abhorrence, contending that the fist was the most natural weapon and by its aid disputes should be settled. That class of man seems to have died out to a great extent, and it is for those who make the manners, customs, and ethics of peoples their peculiar study to determine whether its disappearance is a gain or a loss to the nation.

"Evening Star Monday, December 27 1880

Sudden Death of the Renowned "Tipton Slasher"

Who is it that has not in some period of his existence - especially South Staffordshire people – heard of the "Tipton Slasher"? In the days when pugilism - which we are happy to say has now been almost entirely stamped out – was in its prime, "Tipton Slasher" was a name to be feared and dreaded, but now alas! Death, who makes no distinction between peer and peasant, pugilist or dog-fighter, has claimed his own, and the renowned "Tipton Slasher" has gone to that bourne from which no weary traveler returns. William Perry, alias the "Tipton Slasher", died suddenly at his residence, the Old Toll Gate House on the Bilston Road, on Christmas eve, and so to speak closed his career with the year 1880. William Perry was born on 21st March 1819 in that portion of Staffordshire, Tipton which has been so closely

11

allied to his name for years, not to say to the boast of many of the hardy sons of toil who have ever taken an active interest in sports of every description. *In early years he displayed a propensity for the noble art of self-defence, and many a gallant battle has he fought, in the majority of cases, with victory, and, probably the sporting world will revere him all the more, seeing that, for a considerable time he held the champion belt of England, and it was only wrested from him by the renowned Tom Sayers. Without going farther into the old man's history, suffice it to say that he died suddenly on Friday afternoon, at the ripe age of 61, the exact cause of death being at present unknown. Of late years he has constantly been met with in the district, and in compliance with orders which have made the more brutal pastime illegal, the "Tipton Slasher" has in accordance with rules of the age, confined himself to displays of the art in gloves, and on more than one occasion has he appeared at what the fraternity have dubbed "reunions" for the benefit of some worn out or ill-used - worldly speaking - veteran. He leaves behind him a family, and in the male line they have certainly displayed some of the leading traits of the old man's character, but the time has gone by when they will be able to hand down a name similar to that which the celebrated "Tipton Slasher" possessed."*

I make no apology for reproducing this obituary word for word as it was written by a journalist who obviously saw the great man in action and writes from the heart.

His Life And Times In Poetry

1 Bill Perry lived the life God gave
 He's gone to his long rest,
 We'll write these words
 Upon his grave
 'He fought and beat the rest.

2 A king he was within the ring
 A Songster in Spon Lane;
 No more again we'll hear him sing
 'My pretty, pretty Jane.

3 Ben Caunt has gone
 (of Doubtful worth)
 And Dodging Bendigo.
 And Freeman Bold, of giant Girth
 And fouling Paddock too.

4 Tom Sayers, bravest of the brave,
 Has long ago, passed on;
 Their bodies lie within the grave,
 Their fighting souls box on.

5 That Death! Grim Victor of us all
He found the Slasher tough!
For never did the Slasher call
'Old on, I've had enough'.

6 'Enough, enough!' he never cried,
But battled toe to toe
Unflinchingly his fists he plied,
And Encountered blow with blow.

7 And, if you have a tear to Shed
Friend, let it be a splasher!
And let it fall for him now, Dead,
The gallant Tipton Slasher.

2. A Cartoon of The Slasher From A Sporting Paper Of The 1860's.
It Shows His Shoulder Development And Pads Of Muscle.

King Coal Became God

The Black Country at the time of the Slasher was indeed Black. Day was turned into night from foundries and furnaces which belched out their own poison, filth and squalor. Epidemics of cholera spread though the land with starvation around the corner. Cholera which swept the Black Country was founded upon the evils of putrid water contamination. The landscape was shaped by its pits symbols of its Black Age. By the 1850's coal was mined in almost every part of the Black Country, the rise of pit mounds engulfed the area of green in pastures and orchards. The Black Country was described by outsiders as a scene of dark images and satanic mills.

"WHEN SATAN STOOD ON BRIERLEY HILL,

AND FAR AROUND HE GAZED,

HE SAID "I NEVER SHALL AGAIN

AT HELLS FLAMES BE AMAZED".

Hundreds of citizens in the region were murdered weekly. These murderous times were caused not by war but by mass starvation, poverty and unsafe working conditions. Death in childbirth was not uncommon and the splitting of families was not easy but survival was the only resort.

Let's not glorify the Black Country. Times were hard and degrading. Let us admire the spirit and will power of the men and women who made this region great and whose only way of escape was to meet their maker. Wives pawned on a Monday and re pawned on pay day, replacing their rings with a brass curtain ring. A never ending cycle of pledge and redemption. Strikes were common amongst miners during the 1860's and in 1860 striking miners roamed the streets in gangs ransacking, and looting shops in the Tipton area.

At the beginning of the century only one person in ten lived in a town but soon the new factories and doubled earnings had attracted workers to the town. The result was appalling. Overcrowding in hastily built houses, the well and earth closet (adequate in village life) were lividly insanitary in these conditions. There was no way to dispose of rubbish except by throwing it into the street or a stream – the source of drinking water. Cholera outbreaks soon focused public alarm to the problem. Smallpox, typhoid and gastric fever were rife. The lack of clean water was the root cause of an awful high death rate in Tipton and surrounding towns. The mighty influx of immigrants from Ireland, Wales and the rural hamlets of England put a huge strain on ancient natural water sources. Netherton became the dumping ground for cholera victims as local graveyards were overflowing.

Not only the living but the dead were overcrowded and there was no control over how or where the latter was buried, often they too were in unhealthy close proximity. Protests mounted.

The Dark Regions – The Workhouse

The workhouse cast its own spell of horror over the poor of the Black Country. It was the last port of call before a pauper's grave.

Living on the strap with moonlight flits and to get into debt with no prospects of ever getting straight was a way of the times. The mention of the workhouse sent a shiver down the spine, while the degrading means test was conducted by gentry whose only interest was to keep the poor down. These houses were created with the best of intentions but later plumbed the very depths of degradation. The workhouse master was allowed a sum to feed and clothe the inmates and they were at the mercy of this man only existing by his whim. The young of the house were simply hired out to employers who treated them worse than animals.

Each parish was responsible for its poor and rates were levied for this purpose much to the annoyance of those who could afford to pay them – the middle and upper classes. Families were segregated and forbidden to speak to each other. Children were left to the mercy of the master.

Inmates who were taken in covered a wide range of social outcasts; orphans; cripples; debtors; lunatics; prostitutes. The institute was intended to house and feed those who had no prospect of helping themselves. Entering those doors meant surrendering your dignity and rights.

The great depression occurred between 1874 and 1890 when starvation was rife with the workhouse being the last resort causing families to separate and remain segregated.

In 1883 Mr Andrew Doyle, a Poor Law Inspector, visited the Dudley Workhouse. His report shows "a lack of clean water, overcrowding, a lack of medical attention was evident and privies (outside toilets) so foul that they cannot be used".

The Industrial Revolution brought not only wealth but also great poverty to the area.

A Description Of The Black Country Man And Woman Seen By The Late Rev Percival

"Here men and women cohabitate and propagate with no marriage ties, the man will serve you as a dog, fight for you, or fight your good self if you will but give him beer. This not only applies to the man but to the woman herself who had more manly qualities than the man. The woman of the Black Country found work in the brick yards or on the pit bonk and returned home covered in clay or coal dust to bear children with body racking regularity. There is no doubt that Black Country women of this period work hard bearing, large families. The families who invaded the area brought with them new customs and traditions. A new Iron Age enveloped the area; the separate factions became one while a dialect of old Saxon survives.

To this day women are as tough as the men with Amazonian muscles, smoking pipes, drinking beer and wearing caps, no equality only degradation for them. Most women worked above the ground, while the 1842 Act forbade children under the age of ten from going underground, for generations they were employed from the age of six dragging coal carts through dark tunnels, never seeing light during the winter months.

Charles Dickens wrote of the area, 'A Black Region where not a blade of grass was seen to grow, where not a bud put forth its promise in the spring, where nothing green could live but on the surface of a stagnant pool'.

Before the region and landscape became pitted with mines and air became polluted from the hearths of the forges and with rancid smells of open sewers everywhere the area was a different story. The area consisted of small villages and hamlets where generation succeeded generation without much movement of population."

Tipton – The Birthplace Of William Perry

TIPTON, OR TIBBINGTON is a confederation of canals, railways, furnaces, smoke, and dirt. The parish contains 3000 acres of land. The population increased six fold in fifty years, and amounted to 30,000, beginning at the rate of ten to every acre. Of course this increase must have been mostly supplied by importation; and strength being the chief thing in request, the roughs of many districts settled down in Tipton. Although there were 18 places of worship there, the working people as a body were desperately ignorant and uncouth. The only superiority they bragged of being of three kinds - bull-dogs, prize fighters, and coal - two of the champions of the ring having been cradled here - numbers of celebrated dogs bred and born - and the six ton lump of coal, produced and sent by Tipton to the 1851 Exhibition; this enormous black diamond measured in height six feet, and circumference 18 feet.

Although what may be called Tipton does not extend the breadth nor length more than three miles it is the sinuosity of the Birmingham Canal that exceeds 20 miles within the limits of the parish and affords, in connection with its collateral branches a communication with almost every line of inland navigation, and the produce of its mines and manufacturers was conveyed to many of the principal towns in the kingdom. The coal measure was said to be inexhaustible, the strata averaging 30 feet in thickness and the iron works were on a most extensive scale.

Nails and hinges were made in great quantities, as were fire irons, fenders, boilers, and steam engines, with many other articles from iron. Cannon of large calibre were manufactured at Gospel Oak Foundry. There were also boat building and timber yards, and a considerable manufactory of soap, while clay of a superior quality, obtained here in great plenty, was employed in the manufacture of fire bricks. The land here, from the great value of the mineral treasures it contains was known to be rented so high as £1,000 per acre. Tipton's canal network resulted in a greater density of navigable waterway than any other inland town in Britain and therefore warrants its name of "the Venice of the Midlands". The blood of a hundred bulls had been shed on the clinkers of Tipton Green. If Wednesbury was a town of cock fighting fame, Tipton was infamous for its bull baiting, the sport was banned in 1835 and died out by 1850. The history of Tipton is well known and is famous with firsts. It was first known as the Old Saxon Village of Tibbington. The name refers to the people as followers of the Clan of Tibb. The town's major claim to fame goes back to 1513 when registers first began. These registers are believed to be the oldest in Britain. The registers actually began on December 20th 1513 when a baptism was entered.

Tipton is a town with iron in its soul, surrounded by rich deposits of iron ore and developed by two of Tipton's sons. Tipton iron industry has brought prosperity to the town. Dud Dudley who owned a home in Tipton perfected the method of smelting iron with pit coal instead of charcoal. His discovery had far reaching implications as he paved the way of a worldwide industry. The inventions of Joseph Hall a resident of Tipton for 60 years also had a revolutionary influence, his new method of refining the raw material, known as pig boiling, and a new way of bottoming surfaces pushed the output at the Bloomfield Iron Works from 50 tons weekly to not less than a 1000 tons weekly. The early pioneers gave birth to the many varied products of this iron producing town.

Black Country Entertainments of the day

Bull Baiting was seen as the most barbaric pastime of the Black Country. Tipton was famous for its baiting as bull after bull was killed at the wakes. Bulls would be chained to a stake and Bulldogs would be set loose on the bull, again bets being waged amongst the hostile crowds. Tastes for blood sports were in keeping with the area, the bull dogs ferocity matching its owner. Dogs that missed the tossing horns and stamping hooves of the bull attached themselves to the bulls flesh and dragged the exhausted animal to its knees where death was slow and unmerciful, the tormenting and teasing continued right to the end with death being the only release. His fate was sealed, if the bull did break free, breaking his chain in a mad frenzy, the crowd would scatter trying to avoid being injured. The bull's life was ended by the sharp point of the butchers knife with a slit of the throat the dispatch of the bull was killed thus ending the misery at last. The meat of the animal was sold by the pound to the waiting wives; the only winner being the butcher.

3. Esther with dog

Cock fighting had strong claims to be the period's most widespread sport and ranged across all classes. The cock pits were in general a hurly burly place with frenzied betting taking place, cock fighting or cocking as it was generally known had complicated rules with limitations placed on the interference with the birds by the handlers.

For all the evils in the fighting sport they did play an important role in the making the fights more competitive. Cocks fought in a ring and were paired by weight and trained for their matches not like their human counter parts. Large sums were staked on the contests the cock often had bone or metal spurs (called 'gaffs') strapped to their legs to ensure a fight to the death. Cock fighting began to wane when Acts in the late 1830's against animal cruelty were brought in.

Bull Terriers were bred as fighting dogs and had a reputation of hardness, raw courage and strength. The breeding of these dogs mirrored the times of the area. This is where the Slasher learnt his trade from Toby Duffell, his employer on the cut.

Toby Duffell was described as a rough type who trusted nobody and even when his "licker" had tongued every part of an opponent's dog (to ensure that there was no cheating such as the rubbing in of mustard) he would frequently re-lick the dog himself just to make sure.

William Perry's favourite dog was "Slasher Jack"; a Staffs Bull Terrier who accompanied him in his later years.

The Slasher bred these dogs and was often called upon to referee dog-fights. Hardened miners and chainmakers rarely argued with his decisions.

The Stafford's ancestry can be traced back to the reign of Henry VIII and his daughter Elizabeth. Blood sports were the entertainment of the day. Wakes were held and English Mastiffs were used in baiting. The sport of Bull Baiting led to the development of the breed of Bulldog. Efforts were made to produce a dog that would beat all others, bulls, bears or dogs. In the 19th Century smaller dogs were bred for their agility while still retaining their courage and strength. These dogs are known as terriers.

A Brief History of Pugilism

Pugilism began in England early in the 18th century when James Figg was acknowledged as the first champion of the English Prize Ring in 1720. It was Jack Broughton who had never been beaten by anybody, who decided that a new set of rules was needed to assist in the smooth running of contests. These rules were to govern prize-fighting for almost a century.

Although against the law the new sport became popular with prize fights for money being staged. Big crowds gathered to watch men fight in the roped-off 'rings', usually marked out in a field. Fights went to a finish, that is, until one of the pair was unable to continue. Rounds ended when one of the boxers fell to the ground. When a round ended, the seconds took their men to their corners and attended them during an interval of half a minute. After this pause, the boxers again came 'to the scratch' and set to. If either failed to stand up after thirty seconds the fight was over, the loser being said to be 'knocked out of time' or 'not up to scratch'. Some prize-fights lasted for hours; others ended in a few minutes.

Prize-fighting was a popular spectacle and was responsible for the introduction into our native tongue not just of slang words like 'claret', meaning blood, but of many metaphors still in common use. 'The phrases 'throw your hat into the ring', and 'throw in the sponge', are all echoes of archaic prize-ring practice.

In 1838 a new set of rules were introduced to replace Jack Broughton's Rules and these were known as the Rules of the London Prize Ring or The New Rules .

The new rules of 1838 were an attempt to bring a greater order and acceptability to the sport.

The way in which challenges for fights, details of forthcoming fights and reports of recent contests were broadcast by the sporting press with a newspaper entitled Bell's Life in London (the forerunner of the Sporting Life) appearing to be the number one sporting newspaper.

The newspaper Bell's Life in London not only reported the fights but also provided the publicity which fed and fostered interest in the ring throughout the country but it also during the peak years provided some of those organisational elements which helped pugilism to survive. The editor became the regular holder of the stake money for pugilism and other sports and at times held as much as £15,000 and he or one of his journalistic colleagues also became the most reliable stand-by as referee.

When gloves were adopted for contests (after earlier being used in training), hooking, swinging and upper-cutting were brought into play. Faster and more varied footwork came into use with the springy surface of the modern ring.

Later in the 19th century the prize ring lost the fashionable supporters who had encouraged it in the time of the Napoleonic wars and it fell on bad days. Yet even in 1860 the fight at Farnborough between the English champion, Tom Sayers and John C. Heenan of America, was watched by a large crowd and fully reported in English and American newspapers.

As boxing became less brutal, mainly because of the rules drawn up in 1867 by the 8th Marquess of Queensbury which insisted on such things as padded gloves being worn and other changes to ensure fair play it eventually came to be permitted by law.

4. Tipton Venice Of The Midlands

In Memory of the late Caggy Stevens

"If yo dae fight yo wor in the team"

The Slasher started his life working on the cut and this is where another character was yet to surface in the Venice of the Midlands. The person was to become a Black Country canal legend. A day boatman by trade, he was reckoned to be the last working day boatman in the Black Country. The job refers to one who works

5. Caggy Stevens - Famous Day Boatman Of Oldbury Used To Say Oldbury Had The Best Boatmen While Tipton Had The Best Tatters

boats but resides in a house by night. While life on the cut was not easy Caggy had six working horses and sixty four boats up at Oldbury and West Bromwich. Time was precious and a delay of ten minutes in the morning could mean a couple of hours delay at night.

Caggy took great pride in descending from a long line of Black Country bargees who travelled the teeming and extensive canal network. Caggy was 14 years old when he started working on the cut and covered it many times over. He followed his father and his father's father. Caggy's eating and drinking habits were famous locally. Mad O'Rourke's pub the Dry Dock in Netherton welcomed the lads from Tipton on their Saturday boat runs and where the roof was lifted with their singing. Caggy was noted for eating two Desperate Dan pies – not a flake of pastry was left with the dishes licked clean.

His favourite drink was a pint of beer and a port and brandy; but even his stomach was tested when he took on the challenge to eat a galvanised baby's bath full of crisps without a drop of liquid being allowed to pass his lips. The incident took place at the Old Swan pub in Oldbury and yes Caggy completed the challenge and made the most of the reward of free beer.

6. Geoff Bennet - Probably The Last True Assistant Of Caggy Stevens Working His Tug For Caggy And His Last Horse Tosh Knows More About The "Cut" Than The New Age Boaters With Their Dogs And Polka Dot Hankies. A True Tipton Bloke.

23

The Man

Who was William Perry? What we do know about this man who was courted by Royalty mobbed by crowds wherever he went and was modeled in wax by Louis Tussaud who travelling the wakes and fairs of England exhibited William along with royalty, politicians, murderers and other fellow pugilists. It was said that standing next to William, who in a figure pose, stripped to the waist, brought a blush to Queen Victoria's cheeks. He was described as "a sculptor's dream". His story begins in his birth place of Tipton.

In William's first few years of childhood, he developed rickets - an illness at the time which would have killed one in three children.

The illness left him with a crippled leg which caused the harsh cruel taunts that he endured during his childhood. His working childhood began at the age of seven working the boats on the canal taking nightsoil from Tipton to the Staffordshire countryside. Most children at the time seldom went to school and even 'til the day he died William could not read or write but simply made his mark which was in the form of the "X". There was a class distinction between boat men, and the nightsoil carrier was classed at the bottom. During his time on the "cut", he earned a reputation of "not to be messed with" and at the age of thirteen he had licked most of his challengers for his master Toby Duffell. Toby Duffell was described as a rough tough type who trusted nobody. His hobby was dog fighting and this is where William more than likely picked up the trade as he was known to referee dog fights in his later years. Duffell although hard must have looked after his boys as William at the age of twelve was coming up to six feet and muscled like a man. No man challenged him now for the right to take his masters boat through the locks. Due to his deformity William became known as "Capital K Legs" although I doubt whether they called it to his face. This name stuck with him until his fight with Ben Spilsbury at Oldbury where he became known as The Slasher because of the raining down of round right arm blows in the fight. This name was supplanted later in years to come with the name "Ode Tipton".

In those days the name of The Tipton Slasher was as familiar in the mouths of people as that of any man in England. William Perry, which was his correct name, was born in this parish in 1819; and as he became a native of the "Venice of the Black Country" where he grew up he very appropriately followed the calling of canal boatman. It was in the settlement of disputes with his fellow bargees that he first discovered his own powers with his fists. When presently his fame began to extend, he found patrons in Lord Dudley and Marquis of Queensberry; for at the time Prize Fighting was quite a recognized institution, countenanced and supported by some of the highest noblemen in the land. With rough, honest features; there was nothing in the face of William Perry to denote the pugilist. But he was a Hercules of a man, with enormous shoulders and very peculiar pair of legs. He was knock-kneed to an extent which, if it did not amount to a deformity it certainly shortened his height when he set himself in the attitude of defence with his fists up. In this strange attitude the lower half of his legs were in the form of an inverted V, coming together at the knees, but spreading outward at the feet and practically "sprigging" each other in mutual support. Propped up in this manner he could always wait with confidence for the attacks of the most aggressive antagonist, the solidity of his footing made it well nay impossible for him to be knocked over. As a matter of fact the only one who knocked him clean over was the redoubtable Tom Sayers.

When Perry began his fighting career at the age of sixteen he was nothing more than a big raw lad whose style was of the unscientific "rough and tumble" order. He stood half-an-inch upwards of six feet, and a little later his fighting weight was no less than fourteen stone. Beyond the confines of the Black Country he was unknown to fame, till in November, 1835 he won his first pitched fight by beating Dogherty at Chelsea.

Things That You Should Know About The Slasher

Owen Swift the greatest small fighter of the time and he could punch like a heavyweight, described Bill Perry as the greatest fighter he had ever seen. On meeting William Calcraft executioner to Her Majesty the Queen replied "yoh are the only mon I'd be frittened to meet a second time". Devonshire Randal a useful boxer, on seeing the

Slasher refused to get into the ring with him and later admitted that the look of the Slasher unnerved him.

All reports on the Slasher fights mention the same thing. He smiled good humouredly. If one thing separated the Slasher from the prize fighters of those days it was his handsome face and kind expression.

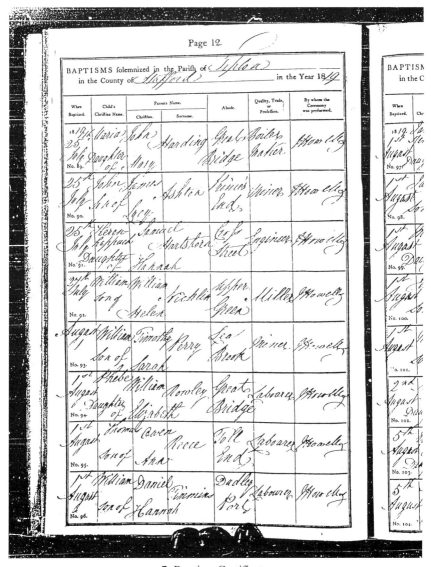

7. Baptism Certificate

Described by a newspaper reporter the Tipton is the last of the great fighters in the tradition of Cribb and Spring. The Prize Ring was declining. No one was left but the Tipton with courage and strength. It was said that when he goes the Prize Ring will die. He claimed that he would beat any man that would stand toe to toe with him in a barrel, with his left hand tied behind his back. He was barred from boxing as fair ground owners feared for their boxers. At one wake he challenged the three resident heavyweights to get into the ring together but so great was his reputation they refused.

It is reported that he once demonstrated his powers on a try your strength machine, much against the wishes of the stall holder. Not only did he ring the bell, but destroyed the machine such was the strength of his punching power. Claims that he could cave a bull's rib cage in with a punch which only travelled four inches could well be founded as bull baiting was a recognized pastime of the local Tiptonians.

The Slasher trained with a large ape, and an interview with Mrs. May Cotton throws new light on an intriguing story. Mrs. Cotton, a direct descendant of Williams' older brother Timothy, recalls the story passed down to her. The ape was killed when the Slasher's father was bit on the little finger by the pet that was consequently knocked down the stairs of the cellar breaking his neck. The ape was kept, after a visit to the local taxidermist, in Mrs. Cotton's bedroom at the Three "Hoss" Shoes. The Slasher's showmanship went with him when he went into the ring and before his fights with Freeman, it is said he entered the ring with a "Davy Crockett" style raccoon hat that he later swapped with Freeman for an eight day clock. In the old Hen and Chickens Tipton exhibitions of clog dancing were held - the Slasher not infrequently satisfying his requisitionists with a display of his drumsticks. His appearance acting like a magnet in filling the house with admirers and curiosity hunters all eager to know the latest movements and future prospects of the Champion of the Prize Ring.

Ben Caunt, Jem Bendigo and Deaf Burke sidestepped the Slasher; for Perry challenged any man in the world and he did not bar weight, colour or country.

It was after his fight with Tass Parker that it was realized that the Slasher was the rightful champion of England. Once again he was lionized and it was written, "for fearless fighting and skill the Tipton Slasher is unsurpassed". The Slasher's foggle, the prize fighter's personal colours was a twenty seven inch square of silk or fine linen. His colours were Black Country Blue Birdseye. Black Country blue approximates to Midnight Blue. The fighter wore the foggle loosely tied around his waist, when he approached the ring stripped for action he or his second would tie his colours to his corner post and this was the sign for a hearty cheer from his supporters. In his heyday the Slasher had been able to catch a fly with his hand, his eyesight and reflexes had been so quick. This quickness went after his fight with Sayers and he would often miss his grip when he hesitated reaching for his pint.

8. Doris Perry

The Perry Family – Doris Perry (One Of The Perry Clan)

Many people claim to be related due to their Perry surname. What do we know of the family? The name "Perry" shows Welsh ancestry. During the 1840s and 50s the name "William" was the most popular name at Christenings. Until this day the name is added somewhere amongst the forenames of the Perry child. His mother is said to have crossed the Shropshire border into England in search of work, with this ancestry giving William a good singing voice.

Many of the boxers have tried to imitate the great man by use of his nickname -never living up to his achievements.

Taken from a London newspaper dated 12th February 1872

"Bare-knuckle battle ends in gaol.

Gentleman Jimmy Maws and Alfred Hawkins (known as the Tipton Slasher) were tonight receiving medical treatment behind bars after a judge sentenced them each to six months imprisonment for participating in an illegal prize-fighting contest. The battle for the British Bare-knuckle Heavyweight Title went fully 23 rounds. In the 22nd round Hawkins was knocked down but Maws blinded by his own blood was unable to see his opponent to press home the advantage thus allowing Hawkins to regain his feet. Finally the referee called a halt when he decided that both parties were too battered to continue. At that point police moved in and arrested the two protagonists."

Extracts From "The Making Of A Novelist" By David Christie-Murray[2]

"I suppose the confession I am about to make will stamp me in the minds of a great many people as an irredeemable barbarian. I care little for that, however, and I am staunch in the opinions which I

---

2 Novelist and journalist. Born in High Street, West Bromwich (1847 – 1907). He recalled his upbringing in **Recollections** where "...there was the most exquisite green fringe to that fire-rotted, smoke-stained, dirty mantle of a Black Country."

have held all my lifetime. Perhaps my voice may find an echo here and there.

I am a lover of the noble art of self-defence, and to my way of thinking few greater blunders have been made by those who legislate for our well-being than was fallen into by the moral people who abolished the Prize Ring. It should be admitted at once that the Ring was full of abuses at the time at which an end was made of it; but it was not beyond mending, and a marked deterioration has been noticeable in the character of our people since the sport of the Ring ceased to be a source of popular amusement. British fair play was a proverb amongst the roughest. The rules of the game were recognized even in a street fight, and the man who broke them was likely to be roughly handled.

It matters that the sense of honour was crude and rough. It was there, and all bullies and blackguards were compelled to abide by it. So long as it was the fashion to fight with fists, the use of the knife, the bludgeon, and the brickbat was far rarer than it is now. The most ignorant crowd could be trusted to police a brace of combatants. There is no harm in a stand up fight with the weapons of nature. Men will fight, and we English people had the least harmful way of fighting of all the peoples of the world. No man was ever good for much with his hands who was not chaste and temperate in life. Excellence in this pursuit was the growth of all the more masculine virtues.

I have the kindliest memories of some of the old heroes. The very first man who helped me on with a pair of boxing-gloves was the mighty "Slasher"- the Tipton Slasher, William Perry, who in the days of my nonage kept the Champion of England public-house and taught me to guard my youthful head; and I have a foolish stupid pride and pleasure in the memory of that fact.

The man had glamour for me and drew me with the attraction of a magnet. I can see him now, almost as plainly as if he stood before me. He was a Hercules of a man, with enormous shoulders, and his rough honest mid-England features had a sort of surfy welcome in his look. But for an odd deformity he would have had the stature of a giant; but he was hideously knock-kneed, and his shamble when he walked was awkward to the limits of the grotesque. You have only to invert the letter V to have an image of the Slasher's legs from foot to knee. His feet were strangers to each other; but his knees were inseparable friends, and hugged each other in a perpetual intimacy. In fighting he used to await his man, propped up in his inverted V fashion, and somehow he gained so solid a footing in that strange and clumsy attitude that he never, in all his experience of the Ring, received a knock-down blow until he encountered Tom Sayers in that last melancholy fight which cost him the championship, and the snug little property in the Champion of England public-house, and his friends and his reputation, and all he had in the world.

But there is no wolf so strong but he may find another to make wolves' meat of him; and Tom Sayers, who had fought his first fight - so tradition tells - on the canal bank within a mile of the Slasher's public-house. He sent in his challenge, and poor old Tipton's colours were lowered for once and for ever… He mortgaged the stock and good-will of the house and backed himself for every penny he was worth, and he was beaten. He was grey and over-fat and his fighting days were over. I forget now for how many years he had held the Championship Belt, but he ought to have been left to rest upon his laurels, surely.

He was dying when I saw him again, and his vast chest and shoulders were shrunken and bowed, so that one wondered where the very framework of the giant man had fallen to. He was forgotten and left alone, and he sat on the side of his bed with an aspect altogether dejected and heartless… In his better days he had liked a glass of Old Tom gin. I carried a bottle of that liquor with me as a peace-offering, and a quarter of a pound of bird's-eye. He did not know me, and there was no speculation in his look; but after a drink he brightened. When I entered the room he sat in he was twirling an empty clay with a weary listless thumb and finger, and the tobacco was welcome… 'The mought ha' let me aloon', he told me, when his wits grew clear, 'I'd held the belt for seventeen 'ear'. (I think he said seventeen, but 'Fistiana' is not at hand, and I can but make a guess at memory.) 'they mought ha'let me aloon, Tum's a good un;' 'I've sin 'em all, an' I've niver sin a better. But he owed to ha'let me be. Theer was no credit to be got in hommerin' a man at my time of life.

All the same, mind ye, I thowt I should ha' trounced him. So I should if I could ha'got at him; but fled hither an' he fled thither, and he was about me like a cooper a walikin' round a cask. An' I was fule enough to lose me temper, an' the crowd begun to laugh an' gibe at me, an' I took to raacin' round after him, an' my wind went, an' where was I then? He knocked me down. Fair and square he did it. Th'on'y time it iver chanced to me. I put everythin' I had o' that fight, an' here I bin.' "

Tom Sayers Last Words On The Slasher

Talking To David Christie-Murray.

"He was the right sort, the Tipton was, and I was sorry to take him down. Perhaps somebody'll come one of these days and lower my colours. It's my turn to-day, and somebody, else's to-morrow."

"I vex the shades no more. Their form of valour is no longer known amongst us; but there are some who regret. I find pathetic among them, and quaint humours, in my memory."

I told Tom that I had known the poor old Slasher, and he spoke of him with respectful sympathy.

The Slasher was the last of the great Prize Ring. Champions he belonged to a world and a way of life that has gone within living memory. When his life and character is evaluated these characteristics stand out, for he possessed them to a superlative degree: courage, endurance, strength, fighting physique, fighting reflexes and fighting spirit.

"AND PERRY BOLD OF TIPTON TOWN, ALL BONE AND MUSCLED MEAT,
WHO SMILING COMES UP TO THE SCRATCH ON FIRMLY PLANTED FEET
AND MOVING FORWARD FIGHTS AND FIGHTS AND CANNOT BROOK RETREAT
WHEN HE IS GONE THE PRIZE RING GOES 'T' WILL DIE IN HIS DEFEAT
THE LAST OLD ENGLISH PUGILIST ONE OF THE OLDEN TIME."

Old Tom Gin

During the Gin Craze of the 18th Century when William of Orange encouraged distillation, London was awash with spirits and the preferred style of the time was Old Tom Gin.

The Slasher was also renowned for his liking of gin. However he preferred the drink Old Tom Gin. Perhaps it was its light sweetness that attracted him to this popular gin known as the "gin of choice" in the late 19th century. Old Tom Gin had disappeared by the late 1950s.

Old Tom Gin was traditionally made from grain spirit and distilled in a pot still with Juniper berries being the most dominant in the recipe.

Juniper was seen as blind allegiance to William of Orange, King of England 1689-1702 who introduced England to Juniper-based Dutch Gin or "Genevre".

Distillation methods in the 18th Century did not produce a particularly clean or pure spirit and initially Old Tom Gin was lightly sweetened to mask any impurities.

The name "Old Tom Gin" comes from what may be the first example of a beverage vending machine in England.

A wooden plaque shaped like a black cat (an old tom cat) was mounted on a wall outside pubs. Passers-by would deposit a penny in the cat's mouth and would be served a shot of Old Tom Gin by the bartender through a tube between the cat's paws.

Hayman Distillers have recently revived this style of gin. The Hayman family has been distilling gin since the 1800s and is the distiller of Hayman's London Dry Gin and Old Tom Gin. Hayman's 1820 Gin Liqueur was the world's first liqueur gin.

The Tipton Slasher

William Perry (1819-1880)

Historical Appendix

8A. Burial Certificate

Although one hundred and twelve years may be conceived of leaving it a little bit late, there was a group of fine Black Countrymen who were saying "It is about time we did summat for the Tipton Slasher!" This concept was not a new idea; in fact this would be the fourth attempt at raising money and spending it in the name of William Perry. He was buried with his wife Anne Marie, to the rear of St John's Church, Kate's Hill, Dudley. The death happened on Christmas Eve 1880. In 1925, the Rev. D.J.S. Mould, Vicar of St. John's, Kate's Hill, Dudley began an appeal to sportsmen of the district to take it upon themselves the duty of restoring The Slasher's grave. Public subscription of five shillings raised enough money to produce a tombstone to mark the spot where the most famous son of Tipton was buried. Again in 1953 a second attempt was initiated, this time by people of Kate's Hill to refurbish the grave of the Tipton. There were others present at the old Freebodies pub meeting of which a firsthand account by Mr. Albert Toe was given. The then Rev. Jones received monies from many a local source, and from as a far as America. Monies were also raised from a Charity Darts Shield contest by local public houses. The early spring of 1992 gave the opportunity for Martin Collinson to take up the Challenge with Jim Holland a local businessman that if something was not done to maintain the grave site to a standard of respect, moves would be taken to remove the remains and resite them in the Tipton Area. Jim Holland was not happy that the Slasher's remains might be removed and retorted "Over my dead body". A compromise was struck between Martin and his band of 'digger-upperers' and Jim Holland that a fitting tribute to William Perry would be undertaken.

34

𝕻𝖆𝖗𝖙 𝟤

The 1925 Appeal -The First Appeal

Tipton Slasher's Grave:-

Dudley Vicar Appeals for its Restoration.

9. St. John's Church, Kate's Hill

The Rev. D. H. S. Mould, Vicar of St. John's Kate's Hill, Dudley, appealed to sportsmen of the district, fittingly to preserve the spot in St. John's Churchyard where lies the remains of that one time famous fighter The Tipton Slasher. The Reverend gentleman wrote "Many Sportsmen of Tipton and Dudley know that in the churchyard of St. John's Kate's Hill is the grave of William Perry, better known as the Tipton Slasher, at one time Champion of England. But few can know how bad a state his grave is or something would surely have been done about it before now. The grave is simply covered by an old iron cage and the name which had been painted on an iron plate is now completely obliterated, so that

35

in a few years unless something is done his grave will be forgotten. This would be a great pity as the Tipton Slasher was a very gallant man and brave fighter, he left behind him a name for courage and sportsmanship and probably the old prize ring was the chief parent of the present British idea of 'playing the game'. It seems to me that the people of Tipton and Dudley might put a stone over the grave by public subscription. Nothing elaborate is wanted a plain slab with an inscription would be ideal. The money might be raised in small subscriptions, say not exceeding 5 shillings, so that it would give everybody a chance to have a hand in the matter. Would some Dudley or Tipton Sportsmen take it up? Obviously I myself cannot find time to do it.'

What do we know about the Slasher's grave? Very little is known. Reports show the grave was surrounded by a wrought iron cage typical to a Black Country graveyard. It is reported that the original monument had been stolen several years after internment.

"100 Donations of 5s[3] Wanted

The appeal made in these columns last week by the Rev. D.H.S. Mould, Vicar of St. John's, Kate's Hill, Dudley, to sportsmen of the district to take upon themselves the duty of restoring the grave of the once-famous fighter 'The Tipton Slasher', which lies neglected in St. John 's Churchyard, has been without effect. Mr. Hugh Corbett, who is one of the leading lights in the sporting world of Dudley and district, is as might have been expected of a man of his generous nature, the first to come forward with an offer of help. At first anxious to open a fund with a substantial donation, but in order to give every sportsman in the district an equal opportunity, he agreed, that donations should be limited to 5s. The cost of a stone slab befitting a man of such mark in the sporting world as was William Perry - that was the 'Tipton Slasher's' name would be about £25, and both the Vicar of St. John's and Mr. Hugh Corbett believe that the sum will be forthcoming. What are required are 100 donations of 5s each, and local sportsmen are appealed to come forward quickly

---

3 5 shillings was equal to 25 pence

with their donations. The Rev. D. H. S. Mould, who is himself an athlete, being a no mean exponent of the fistic art and a good rugby player, is leaving Dudley at the end of September to take up a new appointment near Leeds, and it would be a little compliment to him if the work of restoration could be completed before he leaves the town. It was in a real sporting spirit that the Vicar made the appeal, and but for his letter the grave of one of the greatest local sportsmen may have been lost sight of forever. We respect the words of the Rev. D. H. S. Mould, 'The Tipton Slasher was a very gallant man and a brave fighter; he left behind him a name for courage and sportsmanship, and probably the old Prize Ring was the chief parent of the present British ideal of playing the game'.

With a view of assisting in raising the necessary funds, the "Herald" has, at the request of Mr. Hugh Corbett, agreed to open a fund through these columns, and will act in conjunction with Mr. Corbett in arranging for the work of restoration to be fittingly carried out when the necessary funds are available. Contributions should be sent to the Dudley Herald Office, Priory Street, Dudley, Marked 'Slasher Fund'. "

"Tipton Slasher" Fund

Mr J. B. Bradley, of Dixon's Green, Dudley who was an authority on local history, wrote: -

"I am happy to gather from today's issue of the 'Herald' that subscriptions are reaching you in sufficient numbers to make the success certain of the appeal of the Rev. D. H. S. Mould, the Vicar of St. John's, for a tombstone in St. John's Churchyard to the memory of William Perry, the 'Tipton Slasher' who is buried there. At present the grave has over it only a rose-bush, and a sheet iron memorial on which, as my memory tells me, there was many years ago the name of the departed hero, even then half obliterated, and now completely blotted out by rust and the actions of the weather in this elevated and exposed God's Acre, which must be, I think, from 600 to 700 feet above the level of the sea. I judge from the subscription lists which have appeared in your columns that sportsmen of the town and district have done their part, and I now appeal to those interested in history and literature to come forward and make up the sum needed.

I have sought in vain in the Dictionary of National Biography for any record of the career of the 'Tipton Slasher', and even that more famous hero of the prize ring Tom Sayers, is not mentioned there. William Perry was, however, I believe, a puddler at Tipton, who left the puddling furnace for the fistic arena, and had a very successful career until Tom Sayers knocked him out, and he became Champion of England.

I appeal to local historians because the exploits of the Slasher and his fellow pugilists vividly illustrate the local life of their period and make the dry bones of history live as also do the adventures of the "cock fighters" and "bull baiters", who, at one time, provided so many of the public entertainments of the Black Country. And I appeal to the lovers of literature because Perry has been immortalized by one of our greatest poets in the lines which I quote herewith from Browning's poem."

A Likeness

Or else there's no wife in the case,

And the Portrait's queen of the place,

Alone mid the other spoils,

Of youth masks, gloves and foils,

And pipe sticks, rose, cherry tree, jasmine,

And the long whip, the tandem lasher,

And the cast from a fish ('not alas! Mine');

But my master's the "Tipton Slasher".

November 21st 1925

The "Tipton Slasher's" Grave Restored

It was the late Vicar of St John's, Kate's Hill (the Rev D.H.S. Mould), now of Hunslet, Leeds, who recently discovered the neglected grave of the once famous fighter in St John's churchyard, and who sought the help of the "Dudley Herald" in opening a subscription list for the purpose of restoring the grave sufficiently to perpetuate the memory of the man whose name was familiar in sporting circles all over England. An Appeal for £25 was launched, and the sum was quickly forthcoming from amongst the sportsmen in Dudley and district. Subscriptions were limited to 5s, but one or two odd shillings were sent in with the result that a total of £25.17s was collected. The actual cost of the memorial was £25; the work, which was carried out by Mr. Joseph H. Willetts, of Old Hill; including the preparation of the ground, the building of the stone wall foundation, and fixing a 4in marble slab bearing in imperishable letters the following inscription:- "William Perry, known as the "Tipton Slasher". Born 1820 Died 1880. This Memorial was erected by Public Subscription, October, 1925". The balance of 17s was sent to the Churchwarden's, St John's Church, for the Poor Box. Sadly even then they were mistaken over the year of his birth (1819).

Remembered After A Hundred Years

The 1952 Appeal

"The Rev H. E. Jones, Vicar of St John's Church, Kate's Hill conducted the memorial service to the "Tipton Slasher" in the churchyard on Sunday afternoon.

A crowd of several hundred people assembled in St John's Churchyard, Kate's Hill on Sunday afternoon, for a memorial service to a champion bare fist fighter of hundred years ago - William Perry, known in his heyday as the Tipton Slasher. Jack Holden the ex champion marathon runner read the lesson and unveiled the Slasher's tomb which has been renovated recently. British middle- weight champion Randolph Turpin was unable to attend the ceremony. After the unveiling the Mayor of Dudley Councillor G.S. Marlew placed a wreath upon the grave. Although a number of years ago a Vicar at the Church marked Perry's grave with a tomb, tourists visiting the churchyard to pay homage to his memory were unable to find the grave because the weather had almost obscured the inscription on the marble ledger surrounding it. Through the efforts of a committee who had its origin at (the Freebodies) St John's Road, funds where raised to renovate the grave and refurbish the inscription. The committee was under the chairmanship of Councillor Sam Wright, former licensee of the Freebodies PH, and the treasurer was Mr John Downing a Kate's Hill Undertaker."

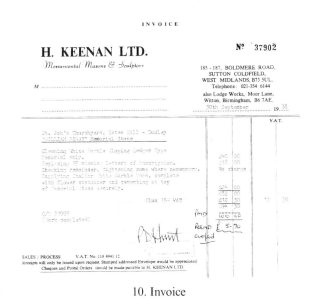

10. Invoice

The Third Attempt

1988 saw the third attempt to tidy and maintain the grave of William Perry. This time by Tipton Amateur Boxing Club situated at the Alexander High School Annex, Queens Road Tipton. The newly formed club entered the Sandwell Marathon with runners in the full marathon and the half marathon. Money from the sponsored run was donated to restoring the grave. The grave itself was described as being in a shocking state, due to these efforts the grave was brought up to scratch.

Part 3

Row Over Plan To Move Famous Boxer's Remains

"A row has broken out over the plans to dig up the remains of the Tipton Slasher from a Dudley graveyard and take them back home. A group of Tipton residents claim the Victorian bare knuckled champion's resting place in St John's Churchyard, Kate's Hill, has fallen into neglect. Now they want to remove the Slasher, whose real name was William Perry, to a Tipton Cemetery where they can look after him properly and erect a statue in his memory. Spokesman for the group said the Dudley graveyard was not a fitting monument to the boxing hero's legend.

He said there was a consensus of opinion in favour of bringing William Perry back to Tipton. "When Tipton people talk about their favourite boxers they always think of the Slasher" he said. "We have made regular visits to St John's churchyard to clean it up and tend to the Slasher's grave but the problem is not getting any better". The move has been blasted by Jim Holland who claimed the Slasher should be allowed to rest in peace. He added the British Trust for Conservation Volunteer's (BTCV) was planning to clean up St John's graveyard. "I don't think that just because the people of Tipton have to catch the bus up here to visit it is a justified reason to remove the remains"

The Return To His Birthplace

Who were the digger upperers? This question has often been asked. What I can gather is that it consisted of Tipton lads who strongly believed in their Tipton heritage and decided enough was enough. Their first meeting was arranged in the Ward Arms Hotel, Dudley and was held in the month of January, 1992. A discussion and agreement was made that the Slasher should be returned to his native Tipton. The name of the digger upperers was taken aboard and so the story begins. A letter was sent to Jim Holland of their intentions regarding the contents of the grave. Such was the outrage that most local papers carried the story on their front page. Late

January saw a meeting with Keith Hodgkins of the Tipton Civic Society to discuss further action; a decision was reached that the removal should remain on hold until further options had been discussed.

3rd March 1992

A letter was sent out to several local bodies expressing a desire that Mr Perry's remains, after 100 years, should be allowed to rest in peace.

5th March 1992

This next meeting was seen as the first step in the beginning of the Tipton Slasher's Appeal, which led to the unveiling of the statue.

The next 12 months saw the founding of the appeal to raise money for a statue. The statue itself was to be placed in Coronation Gardens, close to the Fountain Inn the headquarters of the Slasher.

Little was heard of the digger upperers during this period and it was assumed that they had gone to ground, but had they? During this period strange going's on had been reported in St John's churchyard where the Slasher was buried. Lights and the sound of voices were rumoured to have been seen and heard during this period in what's known as God's Little Acre. One bright spark at the time was quoted as saying "the only spirits they have sin on that bonk is spirits in the bottles in the Freebodies the pub opposite".

Several meetings were held during this period and several major decisions reached. The first and most important was the appointment of a sculptor. Several artists had already added their opinions some of which are listed below. The statue was to be made of fibreglass sited on the side of the canal. Top artists were to be approached. Prices varied and quotes of £40,000 were suggested. William Haynes was appointed as artist and set about his task with enthusiasm and took great pleasure in his task. When queried by a member of the public at one meeting regarding his commitment he replied with a quote of such great magnitude "You are not talking to a beginner, I have the craft and expertise to do the work, one of the few men who are able". And how true this was to be. The statue itself was to be cast in bronze and not cast iron and the target was reached in such a short time that the date of 3rd May, 1993 was put forward as the unveiling of statue.

During this period nothing was heard of the digger upperers, but was more still to come?

Tipton's Iron Man

Little did the Tipton Slasher, the Black Country's great Victorian boxing champion, realise that one day he would be looking at the Jamaican legend Bob Marley and the writer D.H. Lawrence. This unlikely partnership came to pass just outside High Wycombe at the sculpture casting studio's of Burleigh Folds Arts where the bronze statues of the trio where being cast. While Alvin Marriots Marley statue disappeared to Jamaica and D.H. Lawrence went to Nottingham, the Slasher, otherwise known as William Perry (1819-1880), was returned to his native Tipton. The arts world may move slowly generally, but in the Black Country, things are rather different. Remarkably the Tipton Slasher Appeal raised £25,000 and saw the completion of a life size bronze statue created by local artist Bill Haynes in little more than six months. The impressive statue was unveiled in Coronation Gardens. The two men who inspired the project were Martin Collinson

11. Where this story began

43

and Dudley businessman Jim Holland. "My son Ben and my daughter Esther used to come with me to clean up the grave because it was such a mess" recalled Collinson.

"Folks in Tipton were saying 'Now look what's going on - bring him back to Tipton and we will look after him'. That's how the "Digger Upperers" first started".

More care was being devoted to the grave and a fitting tribute was made to the folk hero with the statue project.

The project originated last year when Holland, a subcontractor, went to Tipton for a beer with Collinson, "Some other fellows called the Digger Upperers decided to accost me over the fact Perry's grave had been neglected" he remembered

"The grave is just a few minutes from where I live and I should make the grave my first priority."

"They were determined if we didn't maintain the grave, they would come and dig him up. I retorted 'over my dead body' ".

"But I felt we ought to do something as a fitting tribute to the once Champion of England". They met again and later the statue idea came about and the Appeal was formed.

The appeal had no time for nonsense. A Tipton Silversmith, Bill Haynes, who had trained as a Sculptor at the Birmingham School of Art, attended one of the early appeal meetings, and presented the appeal with a small wax effigy of Perry. Collinson and others were so impressed they asked him to submit a

THE
TIPTON SLASHER

APPEAL

This brochure has been kindly sponsored by

Express & Star
THE BIGGEST NEWS AROUND

12. Appeal Brochure

design for the full commission - and this was accepted. The appeal was launched last October. The reason for the hectic deadline of Spring 1993 was the Statue was seen as a prestige art's project to help launch the Tipton Challenge Programme, renovating this area of the Black Country. The appeal had been given a £12,500 urban aid grant.

While "Brumajum" (Birmingham) debates the merits of such controversial public works of art such as the Mason *Forward* sculpture in Centenary Square and the *Iron Man* in Victoria Square, the appeal decided William Perry should be commemorated with a traditional statue.

"We have tried to make our representation simple"

"You look at it and you say; 'That's William Perry'. It's plain and it's beautiful."

Viewing the completed statue shortly before the final coating had been applied, Collinson was satisfied. "He makes the *Iron Man* look a bit silly - I don't think we could have asked for a better job" he said. The striking feature of the statue is the size of Perry's back and those vast arms. He was a big man – 6ft ½in tall- but was there some exaggeration here? Apparently not. "William Perry was described as having shoulders that were absolutely huge" says Collinson. "When he died his coffin had to be specially made just to get him in." "We want kids to have a good look at the statue because it is part of their heritage". "We are not promoting pugilism. Perry's achievement was he was born the son of a miner, illiterate, but able to get to the top. His achievement is within the grasp of any child from any background - that is compelling".

3rd May 1993 The Slasher's Statue Was Unveiled By The Mayor Of Sandwell.

The unveiling of the statue only 7 months later after the appeal was launched demonstrates Black Country determination on the part of several people reminiscent of the great days of entrepreneurial spirit when the Slasher was champion. It was described as "A great day for Tipton".

13. Bill Haynes

Bill Haynes

The statue sculptor, I for one always had the belief in his ability and whose work will be viewed and classed as one of the seven wonders of the Black Country. Bill is one of the few who can be called a gentleman. Be proud Bill - God Bless ya.

Jim Holland

Stood and fought his corner well and without his help this statue would not be standing in Tipton now. Thanks Jim.

Well did they or day they?

New Grave claim for "Slasher"

SUPPORTERS of the famous Black Country prize fighter William Perry claim that he has secretly returned to his native Tipton. Perry, known as the Tipton Slasher, was buried at St John's Churchyard, Kate's Hill, with his family, but a memorial stone has now appeared at Coronation Gardens Tipton, near a bronze statue erected last May. The stone reads "In these Gardens lie the remains

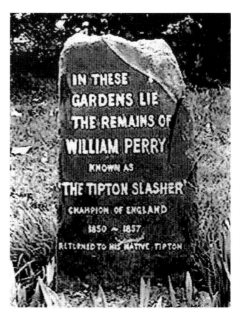

14. The Memorial Stone

of William Perry, known as the Tipton Slasher, Champion of England 1850-1857 returned to his native Tipton". One Perry supporter, who did not want to be named, said the body had been removed by "local lads who decided they wanted to return him to Tipton". He said; "the skeleton hadn't decayed that much because of the lead-lined coffin and the grave was restored so there was no evidence of it being disturbed". The Vicar of St John's the Rev Jim Knights said he was unaware of the grave having being tampered with. Police at Wednesbury and Dudley were sceptical about the claims.

It is an offence under the Burial Act of 1857 to unlawfully disturb human remains.

The purpose of the Act was to control burial grounds. It regulates where and how deceased people may be buried, and provides for the exhumation of remains.

The Act made it illegal to disturb a grave (other than for an officially sanctioned exhumation). Curiously the Act did not make it illegal to steal a dead body, and it is only the opening of the grave which constitutes an offence, not the removal of the contents.

Although claims of the removal of the body are regarded as unfounded photographs were shown to me in 1996 while researching this book - reputedly to be of the grave disturbance in 1993.

What do we know about this Black Country Folklore. Here it is said that the Slasher was reburied in Coronation Gardens, some say under the column where the Slasher stands proud, others say where the memorial stone was placed? Books written seldom give any information about the removal but extracts from talks with one of the lads will throw new light on the stories that surround Ode Tipton. The book has already touched on the subject of the Digger Upperers.

Interview – The True Story – He Doe Sleep In Dudley No More

History if not written at the time becomes changed. Word of mouth over the passage of time alters history. Just one word in a sentence and history is tainted. So after a lot of soul-searching it is time to tell the story of the removal and reburial of William Perry as told to me. Rumours can now be quashed as this part of history is written accurately and recorded for ever. It is now up to you, the reader, to make up your own mind about the story behind a statue.

The year 1992 sees the first mention of the removal of William Perry (not the 70's as reported elsewhere), but it was not until 1993 that the Slasher was so called removed under darkness from Kate's Bonk (Kate's Hill, Dudley) when the following information was obtained.

"I know that most people are arguing that the grave did not look as though it had been disturbed, but I ask you what if the body had been removed late 1992 and not in the month of April 1993 as reported on the front pages of the local paper."

Question. Why was no disturbance found? The grave at the time was overgrown, like the rest of the graveyard, where graves were neglected and hard to find.

Question. How was it that no damage was caused to the grave side? The answer to this is easy. One of the lads was a stonemason, who spent most of his days repairing graves and had kindly volunteered his services. Further local help came from a business man who paid to have the grave repointed.

The question often asked by non-believers is why none of this involvement was seen by passers-by? Simple, Friday night was chosen because of it being payday where the local lads met up in the boozers to quench their thirst and race pigeons, returning home full to the brim avoiding the eerie churchyard.

But there's always one who is exceptional to the rule. Unbeknown to the Digger Upperers it was a short cut for the local wastrel and his only mate (who talked about him rotten) to go home. Shocked on seeing them he said "Bloody Hell lads. Yo'm working late. I hope yo'm on double time." To which he tugged his beard and the two

15. The Wastrel Walk

continued on their way drunkenly bouncing off the gravestones going home.

Was there a scary moment during the removal? Yes two actually. But no one was really bothered when fortified with Tipton Ruin[4]. One can only imagine being in the graveyard at midnight listening to the roars of the lions from nearby Dudley Zoo and when upon reaching the coffin an owl swooped down screeching his warning. This might seem strange but you ask me a question and I give you the answer. Old Bill nearby falling in the grave was a sight to see so I'm told..

What was the second? "Mines a pint of Batham's[5] - me throat needs lubricating with all this talking". The second you ask, well it was another sight to behold, six men running for their lives. Picture the

4 Tipton Ruin – better known as Yates' Australian White Wine – has many names due to its powerful effect on the drinker. It made its comeback in the early 90's and took Tipton by storm.
5 A real ale brewed locally at Brierley Hill. The Shakespearean motto "Blessing of your heart: You brew good ale" appears on the frontage of the brewery tap "The Vine" (known locally as "The Bull and Bladder").

scene, nothing stirring. The only light being from the moon and five lanterns around the grave when out of the dark came the sight of blue flashing lights and the infamous wailing noise. "Quick we've been rumbled" said one of the lads. "Ode Bills here and I doe mean the Slasher." Scattering here and there, it was silly to try and hide as all their tools were left and the sight of the marble slab swinging on the block and tackle was there for all to see.

Well what happened with the Police? Nothing! Turned out to be the local ambulance going out on a job.

The beer had taken its effect. The lad had fallen asleep as usual, face down on the bar. No more stories have been told again - until now.

I still see him from time to time walking down Owen Street, Tipton passed the Fountain Inn. A knowing wink of the eye is shared between us and we both get on with our journeys.

No words are exchanged - only the acknowledgement of us knowing the truth about Ode William and his final resting place at home.

So what are my thoughts on this matter and what is the truth behind the story? I am often asked "Do you have proof?" "Do you have photographs?" No but I have seen photographs in the course of my research including the four sovereigns that were buried with him. The lad even when soddened with drink never changed a word of his story. The police were sceptical. Let's leave it at that, shall we?

16. A Sneak Preview

"Job Done As Promised"- Jack

The Statue depicts William Perry wearing traditional clothing of a bare fisted fighter, knee length breeches and ankle boots. He stands left leg forward and fists raised in a classic fighting pose. Sculptor Bill Haynes, unveiled 3rd May 1993, Designed 1992/1993, Cast in bronze, Duty of Care Sandwell Metropolitan Borough Council, Location:- Centrally in Coronation Gardens, adjoining Birmingham Canal, High Street/Park Lane West, given to Sandwell M.B.C. on the condition that it never leaves Tipton.

The base of the Statue contains two time capsules, not one as stated. One contains a history of Perry's boxing career and a record of the campaign to return him to Tipton, Black Country Newspapers and coins of the realm.

The second was placed in by the late Jack Paskin. He along with Dan Wickett attended daily, come rain or shine, to watch and give advice on the Statue's column. This capsule contains Tipton Amateur Boxing Club's first boxing programme.

Part 4

"It Woe Last Five Minutes" - The Statue Behind The Legend

The quote "It woe last" was from the Tipton bright spark. These words came about when permission was granted for the Statue to be placed in Coronation Gardens.

The Slasher himself had travelled many times between the Great City of London and Tipton, "by the cut", by train, but a stranger mode of travel was yet to come. The Statue left High Wycombe on the back of a lorry travelling along the motorway with people staring at the Champion of England going home, but strange things were to happen. The Slasher lying on his back? Only Tom Sayers had managed this. On arrival at the Gardens the lorry drove past the waiting crowd who had gone for a sneak preview. It was said by the driver that someone other than himself had got control of the wheel and the journey continued down High Street and Owen Street turning around in Albion Street passing the Fountain twice. The Slasher was coming home. The driver was clearly shaken by the whole event. Could this have been seen as a sight-seeing event for the Slasher? Whether the Slasher's quart pint jug was on the Fountain bar full of "old ale" is another story. The Slasher would have approved.

The Last of His Memorabilia

What is left of the Slasher's fighting career is very little. Of his cups, trophies and medals mostly lost when he fought Tom Sayers. I possess one watch chain with a boxing medal. The Slasher's ape resides stuffed in the Black Country Living Museum. Two paintings - one hangs in the Tipton & Coseley Building Society, the other in Tipton Library. This latter one has a chequered history and a direct link to the Slasher.

"Sold as Seen"

So what do we know about the painting that hangs in the boardroom of the offices of the Tipton and Coseley Building

Over My Jed Body

A fermuss mon from Tipton,Lies in a grave that ay respected
It's overgrown, in disrepair and it ay arf bin neglected
He's berrid on the bonk at Kate's Hill; Gods little acre.

If summat ay dun to keep it clane
The digger-uppers ull dig him up again
Yoe cor keep a gud mon down
So they'll bring him bak to Tipton Town

Three chaps called Martin, Jack and Dan
Will berry him in the Coronation Gardins if they can

But ther's a bloke who's nairm is Jim
He ay happy where they'm putting him
Yoe leave him aloon he doe need liftin
His boons can stay theer they woe be shiftin
"Over my jed body" he sed and he wor loffin

"So be it" sed Martin, "Put Jim in his Coffin"
The debate got heated they must compromise
The digger uppers an Jim agree, That would be wise
A life size statue stondin over six fut tall
Is med for Tipton folk and all

On certain days of the wik for a little while
Sum say he sheads a tear and even raise a smile
The Tipton Slasher, He woe be forgot
Cuzz he now stonds proud upon his own plot.

A minature replica of The Slasher I've heard can be seen
Next to the crown jewels of ah most gracious queen
If it ay theer it's bin sed
It's on the terbul by her bed
So raise ya glasses and shout out loud
He was from Tipton and meks us proud

By Peter Hill
2009

Society (TCBS) in Tipton? Well the TCBS hand on heart has curiously never been able to claim that the painting is that of the Slasher. The painting was found behind a wardrobe in a house in the town of Willenhall. It is believed to be painted by Shelley. I have described The Slasher earlier in the book. He had huge shoulders and fists. He was so knock-kneed that the lower half of his legs were in the form of an inverted V. So, was the artist being kind to him by portraying him smaller and without the affect of rickets? I think not. But it set me wondering just who was this gladiator of the prize ring?

17. Sold as Seen   18. Slasher's Corner

Slasher's Corner

There have been several strange sightings of William Perry reported in this corner of the bar at The Fountain Inn, Owen St., Tipton. Oddly this has generally been after closing time by the former landlords. On each occasion the Slasher was sat observing the scene and pondering deep in thought. He was always wearing his smock coat, supping from his quart jug and perhaps wondering what might have been.

Slasher Painting To Hang In Tipton Library

Some say the lion others the leopard, but believe me when a man looks in the mirror he sees the most dangerous and merciless killer in all of nature.

Mrs Cotton tells the story passed on down through the family about the painting and how it got into the hands of the Council. The nephew of the Slasher indeed idolized him and would never see him without drink or "bacca". The painting often being pawned to him and re-pawned back till one day he refused to hand back the

19. William Perry
The Tipton Slasher

painting due to "Ode Tipton's" persistent borrowing and lack of repaying. In the meantime the painting hung behind the bar of the "Three Hoss Shoes" till one day a fight broke out with the painting being torn by a chair leg thrown by an angry customer.

The following information from these minutes is taken from the 1949 Tipton Council General Committee Meeting –

"Oil Painting of the Tipton Slasher:

18 Jan 1949

A letter dated 12 Jan 1949 was submitted from Mr J. C. Fisher of 82 Park Lane East Tipton stating he had in his possession the original oil painting of the Tipton Slasher and that after it had been renovated it was his intention to offer it to the borough as a free gift.

Resolved that this oil painting be accepted by the Council and be hung in the Central Library and that a letter be sent to J. C. Fisher expressing the Councils thanks and appreciation for the gift.

12 April 1949

Oil painting of the Tipton Slasher. The Town Clerk reported that Mr J.C. Fisher had informed him that the oil painting of the Tipton Slasher which he is to present to the Corporation had been renovated and is now ready for handing over.

Resolved (a) that the Mayor be requested to receive the picture on behalf of the committee.

Resolved (b) arrangements for the presentation ceremony be left in the hands of Mayor and Town Clerk.

Resolved (c) that the Mayor's annual allowance for 1949-1950 be increased by £10 to cover the expense of this ceremony. "

Whatever happened to the Ape?

Mrs Elizabeth Harding, was licensee of the Three Horse Shoes whose great great grandfather was related to the Slasher, on her retirement consented to give the ape to a Mr S G Budgen, licensee of the Prince Regent Public House, Tipton. The transfer was arranged by Mr J C Fisher a local antique dealer. It was here that the rumours started that the ape was burned on a bonfire at the back of the pub. Claims that throw a new light on to this story appeared in a local newspaper during 1970 when an ape was donated to the local Museum with claims of it being the pet of the Slasher.

20. Slasher's Ape

The Fights

Dedicated To the Late John Brimble – My Old Sparring Partner

This book would not be complete without a mention of this man. The views expressed are my own. How do you put into words the work that this man did for Tipton? His knowledge was immense and so was his commitment to promote the Borough. I disagreed with some of his views especially where the statue was concerned but my view of this man never changed. A man who offered and gave so much to the town of Tipton.

To a true gentleman a "Bostin Mon"

Salus Populi Suprema Lex

'The health of the people is the supreme law"

21. "Sankeys", the Old Kings Head

The Old King's Head, Dudley Road, Tipton.

The Slasher spent many a night at the King's, later known as Sankey's, sleeping off the effects at the house next door (my great-grandparents' abode)

First licensed in 1818 to a John Smith who by trade was a blacksmith, the King's was to become a favourite haunt of William Perry.

It was here that the betting sting of the Slasher's career started; where retribution was heaped on Johnny Broome and his fellow Brummie bookies with the Slasher and his followers backing himself to lose. The fight was against the Yank – Freeman.

In the early years the pub was famous for its drunken brawls which took place regularly at week-ends between the blokes from Tipton and them from over the Dudley border. Worse for drink they were surrounded by their womenfolk who shouted and cheered their men on. The police simply waited until the battles were finished before acting. Every Wednesday and Saturday horses would be trotted out while the dealers would barter with buyers. Cocks and dogs fought in the back yard. Anything could be sold including meat and fish "borrowed" from the local butcher's and fishmonger's stalls. If you wanted it, it could be got. Friday night was Raffle Night where a draw for a joint of meat was held. It was big enough to feed a family for a wik. The raffler would be kept in a drunken stupor. A fast penny could be earned by the young lads of Tipton as they even sold the "hoss muck" for a penny a barrow load.

Little is known about the King's amongst the gentry of Tipton who gave the pub a wide berth owing to its reputation. Just entering the pub could be a big mistake and many a gent was shown the door (by means of a good old-fashioned "leg and a wing") meeting the outside street with a thud. The Slasher's headquarters was always claimed to be The Fountain Inn, Owen Street, Tipton but he held court at the King's every weekend during his early days and the later days of his reign. With the Slasher in the house training and drinking became a regular habit, swelling the pockets of the pub landlord.

22. Training H.Q. (sadly now demolished) at the Fountain Inn

The Story Of A Legend

At the age of sixteen, William Perry had worked his way to London and was working as a navvy in Battersea Fields and Chelsea. It was here that his reputation came to the fore and his first recorded fight took place. A fight was arranged between himself and a Barney Dogherty on the 3rd November 1835. The local sporting paper described him "Perry is a lad coming up to six feet, his shoulders are truly tremendous and there are great pads of muscles on his upper arms so that his width is enhanced. The handsome kindly looking fellow is a sculptor's model from his waist up but his knees are knocked to a remarkable degree... His speech is uncouth and slow. We are told this is the dialect of the Staffordshire lower orders".

Although this ungainly specimen of a boxing athlete first saw the light, in the year 1819, in the town of "The Black Country" from which his nom de guerre was derived, he came to London and worked in his neighbourhood of Battersea Fields and Chelsea as a "lumping lad" who, despite the drawback of "a K leg" could hit, stop, and use his "fives" with formidable effect. In November of that

60

year we read in a sporting paper "the admirers are milling in the military village of Chelsea, where the "the saloon of arms" of Alec Reid is a centre of attraction, from the arrangement of a "field day" to decide the best man question between two pugilistic heroes of the locality. These were Barney Dogherty, a sprig from the Emerald Isle, and Bill Perry, a young navvy, whose displays with his digits, if not quite scientific, are determined and dangerous. Perry was backed by a sporting butcher, Dogherty by a circle of his enthusiastic countryman. In weight the Emeralder had the advantage of nearly a stone. Each man was waited on by a member of the Prize Ring, and the regulations of the Ring carried out. "The fixture was Wimbledon Common, where miscellaneous groups were seen wending their way at an early hour; but the police scouts where wide awake, and on reaching the intended scene of action it was "no go" and the disappointed crew looked as blue as their enemies. A move became inevitable and new ground was taken opposite the Ship at Mortlake. Here the men set to, but after seven rounds, all in favour of Perry the lobsters were again on the scene and another retreat was made towards Barnes Common. Here also it would not do – the pursuers were on their heels and a helter skelter sort of march took place over Putney Bridge.

Here a council of war was held, and it was at last agreed to march for Lechmere Common, close to the sporting ground of the Baron de Berenger, in the Kings Road. Here all was right – a fresh ring was formed without interruption, and the sport was resumed and concluded. "On squaring elbows there was a good deal of sparring, and Perry dodged left and right. After some heavy exchanges and a rally Barney went down weak. The fight was prolonged for six rounds more, during which Perry had it all his own way, punishing Barney terrifically; still the poor fellow came up as gain as a rhinoceros, and would not give in till his seconds, seeing he had not a chance, cried "enough" and his friends were all satisfied he had done his best to win. "Dogherty turned out to be too stale for active operations; added to which he is slow and awkward in style of setting to. Perry is a scientific hard hitter. The outcome was never in doubt. Perry proved to be a hard hitter who punished his man severely from the start. What most surprised the onlookers, though, was his smartness on his feet, his dodging this way and that to avoid the few blows his opponent managed to launch. While he impressed, some compared him unfavourably "and unfairly, for a beginner" with Alec Reid at his best. At least in the Chelsea Snob's young days such a beginning would have ensured support and further progress to more fights. As it was, Perry became frustrated at the absence of opponents. For weeks he turned up dutifully at Alec Reid's on Tuesday nights, but seems to have found no candidate for his favours for twelve months, and to have worked his way back towards his native place. Here his fame as a fistic practitioner was pretty generally acknowledged, and a party of Birmingham boxers, having among their number Ben Spilsbury, being in the town of Tipton exhibiting the art, young Perry put on the mufflers with that professional. Though the Tipton lad was not as clever as the Brum, he displayed such determination, and got so well "on" to his man, that an observation that, "if in earnest" Mr Ben would have to play second fiddle, led to an offer on the part of a Brum to post a "tenner" upon the experiment. "A friend to sport" at the request of Perry, covered the two sovereigns deposited; and as the Christmas holidays where approaching, December 27th 1836, was named as the day of Battle. After taking some little liberties with The Tipton in opening rounds, for which he occasionally caught a fearful right handed visitation, and was rallied down, Spilsbury started optimistically until he felt the force of Perry's right whenever he came in – his fierce swinging blows meant that from now on he was known as the Slasher. The fight, which ended when Spilsbury quit the ring after nineteen rounds, took place in 1836 on what was becoming a favourite pugilistic occasion in industrial areas. The end of the nineteenth round Spilsbury was carried away and William Perry was left in procession of the field, the stakes and a nickname.

The ring of those days was a place for only the toughest and bravest of men who were prepared to fight each other until they dropped. What matter? The Tipton Slasher had arrived.

Shortly after this he was challenged by Skim Skimmy, a huge Gornal man to fight to a finish according to Gornal fashion. The prize was a donkey and a bag of sand. This may not sound a great deal, but plenty of money was won and lost on the bets. The Slasher backed himself to win with every penny he had. "Gornal fashion" needs explanation. It was fighting as it was before the days of Figg and Broughton. There were no rounds; only kicking and gouging were barred; combatants fought in bare feet and fight ended when one cried "Enough", was unconscious, or was disqualified for persistently fouling. A draw was impossible. The fight took place at Park Hall on the canal side early in 1837 and lasted two days. Many stories are told about it. It commenced at 2 pm and was not decided by 5 pm by which time it was dark. The fighters agreed to carry on at 2 pm the next day when after two hours of fighting Skimmy was unconscious and The Slasher, hardly marked was declared the winner. He cleared about £25 in side bets, sold his donkey and bag of "lily white" sand at the ringside, after which they adjourned to the nearest inn. At this time William was unable to read or white or express himself except in the limited vocabulary of the Black Country boatman. Yet he was a good learner and made a favourable impression wherever he went.

Figg And Broughton

James Figg, considered the first champion bare - knuckle fighter of England under Prize Ring rules, 1719 to 1734.

Jack Broughton champion 1734 to 1750. He devised the first set of rules for the Prize Ring. He is credited with having made boxing (1) a science, (2) a sport of fair play.

Belloil And Blood For Supper

Belloil is an old word which means "severe thrashing". The Black Country Public House prize fights were known as "Belloil and Blood for Suppers". They were more ferocious than the cock and dog fights that lasted into the 1930s with only a courtesy acknowledgment of the Queensberry Rules.

There was no such thing as a draw a hundred years ago. A man backed himself to win with all he had and his backers did likewise. While he was conscious he would not give in and fights have been carried to the scratch, bloody and blind, and draped over each other so that one could find the strength for a last blow and then fall on top. This was the school in which men like The Tipton Slasher and Tom Hickman, of Dudley, were educated. Very few of these gladiators made money. Many died young for they fought until their battered bodies could take no more. The audience had its beer and cheese while watching the show. Nobody wanted to see the noble art of self defence. The fighters were expected to slog it out toe to toe for a shilling a round. Six rounds for seven and six pence.

"From all mine ancient memories

The rust of time I'll shake

Your youthful blood to quicken

And your English blood to wake

I know it only slumbers

Let can't do what it will

The English Bull dog will be

The English Bull dog still"

The Battle of Two Towns

His next fight was against Jem Scunner the Gornal champion for £25 a side and again was spread over two days. The report of the battle is taken from the Police Budget Edition of Famous Fights Past and Present.

It was the evening on Monday, November 20th, 1837, the day on which Her Majesty Queen Victoria opened the royal pomp the first Parliament of her reign. The little town of Tipton in Staffordshire was in a state of considerable excitement. Crowds of rough- looking men, some of them black with the grime of the coalmine and the forge, others ruddy with the stain of the red lead factories, for which the place was then famous, were gathered in noisy groups along the whole length of the narrow street which bears the honoured name of

England's greatest admiral, but they were particularly thick in front of the doors of the Fountain Tavern, in those days, the great sporting house of the place. It is perhaps unnecessary to say that all this commotion had no connection with the interesting event about which all London was at the moment talking. These rough miners, colliers, forge men and factory hands did not care a brass farthing about their fair young maiden queen, or Lord Melbourne, or Lord John Russell, or any one of the distinguished people who had been taking part in that day's pageant in the metropolis. It was very different business which enlisted their interest. It was the fight which was to take place the next day between their own fellow-townsman. William Perry known to fame as the Tipton Slasher and James Scunner, the Herculean and unbeaten champion of the neighbouring town of Gornal.

The Slasher was at the moment located in the Fountain Tavern with his trainer Tass Parker of West Bromwich and the inn was crowded to overflowing with people anxious to get a glimpse at their fellow-townsman and see how he was looking, for he had come up that day from his training quarters at Buxton, and his friends had not had sight of him since the match was made a month previously. There were a good many Birmingham sportsmen also present – for the hardware capital is but eight miles distant – eager to pick up a tip for the morrow for the Brums had wagered largely on the event, which most of them considered a moral victory for the Gornal man upon whom odds of 7-4 and even 2-1 were freely laid.

Mr. William Perry with Tass Parker by his side stood behind the bar and exchanged greetings with his admirers, who were delighted to see him looking so well and in such excellent spirits. No secret was made about the trysting place. Everyone who chose to ask was informed that at Gospel End, between Wolverhampton and Bridgnorth, some miles from Tipton, the ring was to be pitched at eleven o'clock the hour. As one lot of excited men squeezed their way out of the door, another gang pushed their way in to gaze upon their admired hero and wished him good luck on the morrow, for they in their thousands would put their shillings and half crowns on him. The steam of incomers was perpetual and seemed never ending. The Slasher grew quite tired of shaking hands and answering queries about his health and at last Tass and his pal, mindful of the hard day's work before them went off to bed, but still the bar and taproom remained choke-full of these rough sportsmen, noisily discussing over the liquor the probabilities of their man winning, until the time came for closing the doors of the Fountain Tavern.

A similar scene was being enacted the same evening a few miles off at Gornal, where the principle hostel, the Green Dragon was besieged by a mob of anxious inquirers after the health of Mr James Scunner who is putting up there for the night with his trainer Bill Owen, alias Gallit, a well known Birmingham "pro" and Surrender Lane, who was to esquire him in the ring. James Scunner was a gigantic young forge man over six feet in height and of immense strength. Those who had seen him fight declared that a blow from his fist was like a kick from a shire horse. His fame spread all round the countryside- indeed, to hear people talk one would have imagined that there never had seen such a Nasmyth-hammer sort of pugilist seen in the ring before and that it was useless for any man in England attempting to face him.

FLOORED TWO OF THE ASSAILANTS RIGHT AND LEFT.

23. Slasher steps in

There was one person, however, who despite all these exaggerated reports of Scunner's prowess, did not believe the Gornal champion to be invincible and that was Bob Watson, the landlord of the Railway Tavern, Manchester Street, Birmingham. This worthy Boniface was firmly convinced that they knew a man who would lick this tremendous giant and, having the courage of his opinions, offered to match William Perry, the Tipton Slasher, against him for £25 a side. His acquaintance with the Slasher was made under peculiar circumstances. On returning from a fair in the neighbourhood of Birmingham with his wife and daughter he was set upon by three half drunken men who would have doubtless committed some brutal outrage had not young William Perry, who was passing, come to their rescue and floored two of his assailants right and left whilst the third took refuge in flight. From that day till the day of his death, Bob Watson was a firm friend of Bill Perry and soon proved his friendship and gratitude by backing his portage against Ben Spilsbury of Ashted whom Perry thrashed to pieces. It was from this great determination of character he exhibited in this contest that he gained the soubriquet of the Tipton Slasher by which he was ever afterwards known throughout his long and honourable career as a prize fighter- a career extending over twenty years and culminating in the Championship which he won by his victory over that fine, resolute fighter Tom Paddock. The belt, indeed, was wrestled from him temporarily by Harry Broome in 1851, but Harry preferred paying forfeit to fighting in the return match, and the Slasher continued, undisputed Champion of England until that memorable and disastrous 16 June, 1857 when Tom Sayers "the baby" as Perry contemptuously called him, humbled the pride of the poor old Tipton, then long past his prime, and despoiled him of the trophy which he had won so worthily and held so long.

The Battle Begins

On hearing this task about the wonderful Gornal Champion, Bob Watson found out the Slasher who was working at a forge in his native town and found Perry quite willing to take on the Goliath of Gornal, opened negotiations with Scunner to that effect, the result of which was a match for £25 a side to be bought to an issue on Tuesday, November 21st 1837. So great was the miners, colliers, forgemen, puddlers, potters and craftsmen of all kinds flocked in hundreds from Birmingham, Dudley, Wolverhampton, Walsall, Wednesbury, West Bromwich, Cannock, Brierley Hill and a dozen more outlying districts.

Working at a Forge in His Native Town.

24. Working at forge

The ring was pitched by Harry Potter the well known Commissary of the Midlands and the outer enclosure was beaten out and kept by a number of local bruisers. The Tipton was first on the ground walking up to the ring with Bob Watson, followed by his seconds. The Gornal Champion strode alone to the ropes, his huge form towering over all whom he passed – a whopper and no mistake, and it was not until he had been waiting the several minutes did his seconds put in an appearance. The respected Mr George Everard a publican of the Peacock Inn, Wolverhampton was appointed referee and without further delay the men entered the ring, and retired to their respective corners to strip for the fray. The Slasher sported the time honoured blue birds eye which he used as his colours in all his battles from first to last, but Scunner had no emblem at all, so the usual ceremony of fastening the rivals standards to the stake was dispensed with, much to the disgust of whose who liked to see everything "according to Cocker".

Whilst the preliminaries were being settled, the row around the ring was awful. The interest of the spectators was beginning to centre exclusively on the professional combatants and there was nothing to detract from the enjoyment of the day's sport. For a mid - November day, the weather was fine. There was no sun but the air was mild and there was a pleasing absence of fog. Seven to four on the Gornal Champion were the current odds and they were being bawled out all over the field as two men, in obedience to the referee's signal, walked from their corners to the centre of the ring and having shaken hands with grim politeness, put their hands in double quick time.

Certainly rumour had not lied when it credited Jem Scunner with gigantic proportions. He was nearly, if not quite as big, as Ben Caunt- stood 6 feet 2 inches and weighted, it said, close upon 14 stone. His face and arms were covered with freckles, his hair of fiery red, both on his head and on his vast chest; he had a covering of hair as thick and shaggy as a highland bull's. The limbs of the man were immense and extraordinary brawny and muscular; but there was a looseness about his shoulders, broad as they were, which suggested that the terrific hitting power of which so much had been heard of was no myth.

The Slasher was a big man too, but he looked small by comparison with a man mountain opposite him. Perry who was now still only 18 stood six feet and half an inch and weighed in on this occasion around 12 stone. But except so far as his height and legs went, the Slasher was a very different looking man in 1837 from what he was twenty years later. His frame had not yet filled out into the colossal proportions it afterwards attained though he was even then remarkable for his huge shoulder blades and his face as yet was smooth. Owing to the slouch which his crooked leg gave him, the Slasher did not look his height and when Scunner stretched his long arms, the disparity was etched in the faces of Perry's backers.

The Tipton was the first to get work, trying a "feeler" with his left at the big 'uns body. Jem scorned to stop the blow, but with one mighty sweep of his right caught his man on the neck with such force that Bill was within an acre of being knocked off his legs. This was a caution to the Slasher to look out for squalls, and a gentle reminder that the Gornal Champion could hit when he chose. Following up his blow, Scunner again attacked his man, missed him with hands in his hurry. Loud cheers from the Gornalites and offers of 2 to 1 on Jem, which was taken by several of Perry's backers, who had already seen enough of Scunner's style of fighting to convince them that if the Slasher only kept steady and did not lose his head he could not fail to get the best of such an awkward and unscientific adversary.

The Rounds

The Gornal Champion came up in the hot haste to fight and charged at Tipton as if he meant to annihilate him. But Perry swung himself round on his crooked leg which he was always able to use as a pivot for turning his body just as he pleased, and by that motion placed himself broadside on to his antagonist as he rushed past, giving him the same right handed jab on the jaw and nearly tumbled Scunner over, big as he was. The big "un" as soon as he could stop himself- for the impetus of his weight was no easy thing to check- turned and made another go for his man. This time the Slasher coolly waited for him and gave him one from the hip straight on the nose that pulled Master Jem up very short. He had probably never had such a snorter before in his life and evidently didn't like it. Shaking his head like an angry bull, the Gornal man went full tilt at the Slasher, but was met precisely with the same reception, a stinging left hander on the nose which made him snort with pain but didn't altogether stop him, for he forced his way into close quarters, despite a smack in the mouth and another in the pit of the stomach from the Tipton and clutching his adversary by the shoulder pulled him over by force.

When the big "un" rose to his feet, the blood was plainly seen running from his nostrils and with a loud cheer, the Tipton men hailed the first event for their pal. There were no more two to one offered by the Gornalites now; they were as mute as mice so far as wagering went, though they cheered the man lustily enough and wouldn't even take level betting. Scunner looked puzzled when he came up for number three and instead of charging as before, walked solemnly round his man with his arms well out in front of him to repel any sudden attack on the Slasher's part. Perry grinned at him but made no attempt at assault; he wasn't sure enough of his man to do that yet and he felt that it would be rash to throw away the slightest chance against a man so much heavier and more powerful than himself. Revolving on his pivot leg, he kept his front to the foe and had his left all ready to shoot the big "un" in the face if he tried one of his rushes.

At last Scunner put down his hands and walked to his corner amid jeers and cries of "he's had enough of it", where he asked Surrender Lane for a drink of water. Having rinsed out his mouth the giant returned to the fight where the Slasher was patiently waiting for him but to the amazement of everyone and probably the Gornal Champion most of all. Bill gave a sudden spring and landed his left heavily on Scunner's right eye following up the blow with a scorcher in the pit of the stomach from his right; which fairly doubled the big "un" and he dropped on his knees with both hands clasped over his stomach writhing in pain. "Put your hands on the ground or he'll have you again" shouted Surrender Lane but Perry without waiting for his antagonist, this to make himself technically "down" turned his back and walked to his corner, scorning as he ever did, to hit a man when he was helpless. Loud cheers greeted this manly act of forbearance on the Slasher's part who was one of the fairest fighters ever seen in the ring, and his friends now offered 6 to 4 on him. But the Gornalites were still sanguine. "Just wait till Jem gets one fair crack at him and then it'll be all up with your Slasher" they said and watched eagerly for the sledgehammer blow which was to settle Perry.

But they watched in vain for the awful blow never came. The big "un's" nose which was now the colour of beetroot was evidently very sore and he had no mind to be dosed again on the sensitive point; so the fourth round and the fifth and sixth went by without producing the blow which was to electrify all beholders. It was not for want of trying that the Gornal Goliath failed. Several times he screwed his courage to the sticking point, made one or two of his furious attacks sweeping round his right as in the first round but Perry either met him flush in the face with a slashing left hander or neatly avoided him by springing to one side, as he did so touching Jem up smartly about the ribs with his right.

"Catch hold of him, Jem" roared some of Scunner's friends. "close with him and fling him". Twice the big "un" attempted to do this, but the Slasher twisted himself away so that the Gornal man overbalanced himself and fell. It was clear now that Scunner was grossly overrated as a fighter, he had no knowledge of boxing, no notion of ring craft, rarely even hit straight, most of his blows being rather backhanded chops or round handed "mows"- the man depended solely upon his enormous physical strength and no doubt had he been able to land one of his terrific swinging blows on the side of the Slasher's head, the result would have been serious for the Slasher.

Betting was 2 to 1 on Perry when the men faced one another for the seventh time. Scunner whose face was now much bruised, looked very savage and without a moment's delay hurled himself upon his foe. The onset was so sudden, and the impetus so great that, though the Slasher met his man with another slap on the damaged nose, he was borne backwards by the rush; and Scunner gripping him tightly by the right arm with his left tried to bring his formidable right to bear; but at this moment Perry who was perfectly cool, hit the big "un" such a chop under the chin with his left that he let go of his hold. Thereupon, the Tipton whether from the force of his own blow, or from a sudden jerk of Jem's arm, or from catching his foot in a tuft of grass went flop to the ground in a very peculiar manner. To anyone at a distance from the ring, it certainly had all the appearance of a deliberate drop, and Scunner's friends were evident of their opinion for, with one accord, they yelled "Foul, foul he fell without a blow".

The Slasher turned to the referee and indignantly denied that he had done anything of a kind. But this did not satisfy the Gornalites, they made a rush for the ring crying "Jem has won", "Hooray for Gornal", cut the ropes and without waiting to hear the referee's decision seized their big champion and bore him in triumph out of the arena despite the ring keepers attempt to beat them back.

Meanwhile, the referee on being appealed to decide that there had been, so far as he could see, no intentional foul and ordered the men to go on with the fight. The Slasher was ready and stood waiting in the ring with his arms folded, but Jem Scunner refused to come back, his friends persuading that the claim of foul was certain to be sustained, and he had fairly won the fight.

BORE HIM IN TRIUMPH OUT OF THE ARENA.

25. Bore Him in Triumph

The din and confusion now became so terrible and distracting that it was impossible for the referee to make his orders heard. The ropes were cut, the stakes trampled down, and it was evident that the fight could not possibly be renewed that day in the excited state of the crowd. Mr Everard told Perry that he must come round to the Peacock Inn at Wolverhampton, and there in peace and quietness, they could discuss the question and decide what was best to be done. A similar notification was conveyed to Scunner and so amid a scene of riot and uproar impossible to describe the company broke up. Both Perry and Mr Everard had narrow shaves of being roughly handled by the infuriated Gornalites, but the Tipton's pals rallied around him in strong force and drove the enemy back. . The free fight between the two rival hosts lasted two hours or more after combatant seconds, umpires, and referee had disappeared from the scheme.

Later in the day, both parties met at the Peacock Inn, Wolverhampton, when Mr. Everard had the evidence on each side laid before him, considered it carefully, and finally gave judgement that in his opinion, Perry had not gone down deliberately to avoid his antagonist's blow, that no foul act, therefore, had been

73

committed and that the men must meet in another ring the following day and fight the battle out. He named Kingswood, near Wolverhampton, as the trysting place and ordered both men to be in the ring there at eleven o'clock the next morning.

Let Battle Commence

As may well be imagined, the excitement in Tipton and Gornal and the neighborhood was greater than ever. The public houses were filled with noisy groups, eagerly discussing the pros and cons of the affair over the liquor. Was the big "un" beginning to get the best of it when they left off? Would he have won had they gone on? What tactics would he adopt on the morrow? Would he try the rushing game, or would he play cunning, waiting patiently for a chance of putting in one of those terrific blows (like the renowned Gasman's whisker hit) for which he was famous? The Tipton men were quite confident the Slasher would win. Indeed they declared Scunner was really a beaten man when the fight was stopped, that he flunked the Slasher's facers, and was afraid to go on lest he should be smacked on the nose (his tender point). Consequently, he must soon have been at the mercy of Bill Perry, who could have done just what he pleased with him.

But the Gornalites were of a different opinions, they said their man was a trifle puzzled and bothered first on being opposed to a boxer whose style was different from any he had encountered before, but that he would rapidly have got over that feeling, and calm and coolly put in one or two of his sledgehammers hits any one of which would be enough to knock the fight out of twenty Slasher's. it was a foregone conclusion for the Tipton and 5 to 1 on Perry could have been had that evening at Harry Preston's, Arthur Mathewson's, John Tailby's or Bob Watson's from anyone who had witnessed the fight.

The Second Day's Battle

In obedience to the referee's instructions, both men with their seconds and friends showed up at Kingswood before eleven o'clock.

Harry Potter having formed a fresh ring there an hour or two previously, with an outer rope enclosure of double extra strength, calculated to resist any ugly rush on the part of the Gornal man's partisans. The ring keepers too were doubled in number, and every precaution was taken to secure a fair field and no favour. The crowd was bigger than ever but, strange to say, much more subdued than on the previous day- perhaps the hard knocks given and received in the free fight had the effect of abating the enthusiasm of both parties.

The Slasher turned up as a fresh as a daisy without a mark upon him, but the Gornal Champion's visage was considerably altered, spotted with deep red and blue patches, the lips swollen, the nose ditto, and of a purple hue as well, whilst each eye was decorated with a mouse. There was a very forbidding expression upon Scunner's face as if he meant to make himself as nasty as possible and "savage" the Slasher if he could not settle him any other way.

Just before the set – to Tass Parker, who had been scrutinizing Scunner very closely shouted out "Stop" What's the Gornal chap got in his hands? A bit of lead I guess, or summat o' that sort.

Mister Referee, make him open his hands!"

"Surrender!" Lane declared that his man was all right and added "Never yo mind Jem, you go to work". Whereupon Tass went up, seizing by the arm, led him back to his corner, and said he should claim "foul" if Scunner refused to open his hands. Very surely, the Gornal man unclenched his fists for the inspection of the referee, who found that in each hand was a quantity of powdered resin. "Surrender!" Lane maintained that this was perfectly fair, and could not be called holding a weight to give extra force to the blows. Tass Parker on the other hand asserted this was a foreign substance in the words of the Prize Ring rules, and was not allowable. There was a short sharp wrangle and then as Mr. Everard decided that the resin must not be used in that way, Scunner reluctantly threw it away.

As soon as this little excitement was over, the big'un at once set all doubts at rest as to the tactics he meant to pursue, for he went at his foe like a mad bull - head down, and whirling both arms round like a windmill gone out of its mind. The Slasher who was more self-possessed than ever, calmly waited for him, shifted cleverly on his crooked leg, and let Master Jem have such a smack on the side of his head with his right as precious nearly tumbled the giant off his perch. He was round again directly, however, face to face with his opponent and charged as before, but was hit back with a slashing left hander on the nose, which drew the ruby profusely. With a snort of fury Scunner pulled himself together and clashed at his man in the same reckless style, but Perry's left caught him smack between the eyes and set him back, foiled and half stunned. The Tipton was a much straighter hitter in his early fights than later in his career. His quick lashing blows were a treat to see, for he was looser about the upper works that in his Champion days, when his huge muscles, somewhat hampered him, and like all very strong men he was apt to round.

Once more the big'un made his wild charge, but the Slasher this time slipped to one side and, with a backhander on the neck, sent Scunner sprawling on his face. Five to one on, the Tipton whose friends cheered him lustily as he walked to his corner - a compliment which he acknowledged with a wave of his hand. The next five rounds were precisely similar. Scunner continued his headlong assaults, but was hit back every time with great severity, 'till his face and body was bathed in blood.

After the sixth round, afraid to face any more straight deliveries and fearful uppercuts of the Slasher, the big'un took to outfighting, keeping a respectful distance and hoping to tempt his foe to attack him. But he fared little better at this game than the outer for the Slasher boldly went up to his head sending home his swift arrow-like blows and getting away before Jem could bring round his ponderous fist which he swung like a hammer.

Once and only once did the Gornal Champion get home an effective hit, and that was in the seventeenth round when the Tipton's foot slipped in getting away and he caught a rouse on the back of the neck which made him stagger. For this the big "un" was frantically applauded by his pals who yelled "Another one like that, Jem and the fight's your own". But Scunner had already half the courage hit out of him by the Slasher's hot un's and from this time forward he made more use of his legs than his fists, retreating every time that Perry advanced, and not once standing up for a fair exchange of blows during the next half a dozen rounds. It is only fair to the Gornal man to say he pursued these tactics by the advice of his seconds, who thought in this way to tire the Slasher out and might quel his onslaughts with some hope of success.

In the twenty-fourth round Scunner, whose friends did not approve of his strategic movements to the rear shouted to him to go on and hit away when the Slasher attacked, but he was not in it. With one dreadful blow on the mouth, the Tipton knocked him clean off his pins. This was the first knock down blow delivered, and so two out of three events were already booked to the Slasher.

In the next round Perry hit his man twice, closed and, to the surprise of everyone, threw the big "un" easily. Scunner no more attempted to retreat, but stood to his guns manfully- leaving it to the Slasher however to open the attack every time. His gallantry, however, was all in vain; in every round he was either thrown or knocked down by the Tipton, who now felt he could do just what pleased with the man he had before him.

At last, in the thirty-first round a terrific blow on the point of the jaw from which Perry's right sent the Gornal Champion down to rise no more that day. At the call of "time" which was taken up excitedly repeated by hundreds of voices all round the ring. Jem Scunner was found unable to respond, for he lay insensible across Surrender Lane's knees, his eyes closed, his mouth open, the blood running from his nose and two big gashes on

Both Hands Clasped Over His Stomach, Writhing in Pain.

26. Down He Goes

77

either cheek, his face dreadfully battered and bruised. So, William Perry, the Tipton Slasher was proclaimed the winner of his third consecutive victory, the battle having lasted exactly one hour.

The Gornalites were very savage at the defeat of their Champion and the Tipton men gave the winner an ovation as he washed and dressed in the ring. At one time there appeared to be a likelihood of a serious riot, but the mob contented themselves with sacking a public house which stood near the common, and then dispersed noisily indeed, but without further bloodshed.

Floored His Foes in Rare Style.

27. The Gornalites

On the arrival at home, the Tipton received a most enthusiastic welcome. At one bound, he leapt into fame, for his victory over the Gornal Champion was rated far more highly than it deserved owing to the great reputation which Scunner bore. The man knew nothing whatever about fighting and the Slasher never had an easier job in his life than of licking this gigantic imposter, but the people in those parts did not see it in that light. Bill Perry had thrashed a man who was reckoned to be the most formidable fighter that had been seen in the Black Country for many years, and without troubling themselves to inquire what claim Scunner had to be regarded as a phenomenon they elated the Slasher at once into a popular hero. For the next fortnight and more, he and Tass Parker were lionised wherever they went, and when they took their joint benefit at the Fountain Tavern, hundreds were turned away from the doors after the room was crammed to suffocation.

Tass and the Slasher after this went on a starring tour throughout the Midlands and met with an enthusiastic reception at every town they visited. Little did either of them think then that a few years later they would meet twice as antagonists inside a twenty-four foot ring and be as bitter enemies as they were now firm friends.

As to Jem Scunner, the Gornal Champion, nothing else was heard of him outside Gornal where his broken backers for many a long day indulged in mourning and lamentation and woe over the painful memory of the disastrous day which had witnessed the humiliating downfall of their Champion and the heartrending loss of pots of money they had so recklessly wagered on him.

After this defeat Scunner became gatekeeper to a Noble Lord.

A benefit was arranged and held at The Fountain Inn - a hostelry that was described as "Perry's personal tap".

28. Police Budget Edition

Famous Fights Past and Present

View point from outside the ring from an old boxer after the fight with Jem Scunner.

"Admit it there's something in the young man's eye that would make any one of us step back. What I see in him is a dangerous animal who wants the taste of blood."

What follows features eye witness accounts taken from the Police Budget Edition of Fights Past and Present; Pugilistica Boxiana; Bell's Life & Giants of the Ring.

The Slasher had many fights both in the ring and out. Many were not recorded but these fights are taken to be a record of the Tipton's rise to fame.

Tom Langley reports in his book:

"The Bell's Life reporter never gave the Slasher a good press, why? The answer can only be conjectured and now no longer matters."

A new Name for the Slasher

December 1837, William had many nicknames but now we come across a new name for William, where a challenge from John Farnell of Wednesbury, to meet the "Tipton Bullock". "Who had just defeated the Gornal Miner" for £50 to £100.

25th May 1838. The match has been made between the Tipton Bullock and Farnell. The money for the match can be seen at S. Parkers, Old Meeting Street, Wednesbury.

One fight the Slasher would not take on was with Elijah Parsons (The Punching Preacher) from Wombourne. Bill was a complex character and refused to fight a man who day drink, cuss and swear or never "gozz a wenchen". A strange principle for a bare knuckle boxer.

Infamous Dealings by the Brum

The defeat of Jem Scunner, who had an immense, though underserved, local reputation, in a period when the dearth of good big'uns was remarkable, spread the fame of the prowess of the Slasher so widely that he was fain to wield the shovel in laborious obscurity, instead of flourishing his ponderous mauleys in the 24 foot. In the interval, "the Deaf un" had returned from Yankee land, and - despite his two successive defeats by Bendigo (Feb.12, 1839) and by Nick Ward (Sept.22, 1840)- owing to Bendigo's accident, and Caunt's announced absence in America, boldly claimed the Championship. Johnny Broome hereupon sought out the Slasher, calling to his aid some patrons of the Rising Sun, he proposed a "trial by battle" to settle the difference of opinion. Burke's backers came to the scratch with their rhino, for a battle to come off in August, 1842, but at the fourth deposit Broome thought fit to absent himself upon the nigh of "posting the possible" at Owen Swift's, and the Slasher's money was confiscated to the extent of £15.

The Tipton, as we know, was a mere tool in this affair, as in other instances, of the over-cunning Johnny Broome, who, like most self-sufficient sharps, often "cut before the edge".

Johnny had other views of the "dark horse" which he flattered himself he had in his own stable, and, as he didn't find the money, the poor Tipton suffered in reputation (as Johnny intended he should do) by this forfeit. The Editor of Bell's Life, too honourable himself to suspect this double-dealing, observes: "Though Broome was certainly late, this insistence on forfeit seems very sharp practice; the more so as the same gentleman who backs Perry actually assisted Burke with his deposit. The forfeit, however, has yet to be taken by Burke's backers, as he has nothing to do with it beyond their approval, and we may yet find that the last and remaining deposits will be posted, and "the ball go on". We have since received a letter from the gentleman who put £4 of the first deposit down on behalf of Burke, when the match was made, starting that he will not consent to the forfeit being received, and expressing his desire that the match may proceed, as his only wish is to encourage the manly sports of the Ring".

Johnny Broome was comfortably married and settled as a prosperous tavern-keeper in the capital. Always alert to pugilistic happenings on his native heath, he had noted the Slasher's achievements, but three years passed before he saw an opportunity that appealed to his devious mind. Burke was tied up first with Bendigo and than with Nick Ward. Bendigo went down with injury and Caunt had decamped to America, and Broome saw no profit in dealing with less fry. It was a further lesson in contemporary ring affairs, where the exchange of actual blows in the ring was a very occasional and minimal part of the whole business.

Johnny Broome had, in fact, been seized of a notion that promised greater profit than a doubtful encounter between his raw, wild-hitting novice and the strong, skilled and tried "Deaf" Burke, even if he was now well past his best. What Broome eyed with envy was the success that Ben Caunt was enjoying exhibiting with the gigantic

American, Charles Freeman, whom he had brought back across the Atlantic. Freeman, 7ft, tall and 20st, in weight, had no ambitions to become a prize-fighter, and his "sparring" with Caunt, which was packing the theatres and assembly halls, was little more than a caricature of boxing.

However, some theatre managers indulged in the most extravagant publicity, even proclaiming the innocent Freeman as "Champion of the World", ready to meet any challenge. It was a chance that Broome would not let slip. With equal theatricality he threw down a challenge on behalf of an unnamed "invoice", the stakes to be £100 a side. Freeman was prevailed upon to accept, and the usual long string of preliminary meetings to build up the stake money took place - eight further engagements, at Johnny Broome's, Johnny Walker's, Jem Burns's and Tom Spring's. It was a process which allowed more time for the often difficult task of building up the stake money, extended the excitement and the publicity and brought some welcome business to the sporting publicans. Both fighters went into serious training. Freeman's regime included walking twenty to thirty miles a day, which, by reducing his excess weight, only served to make his Herculean figure the more imposing. Its symmetry, despite its enormous size, was much admired. Widespread interest was aroused by the coming contest and the debate on the relationships between size and strength extended into serious medicine, with an eminent surgeon subjecting both men to a series of tests on lung capacity, respiration, pulse rate and muscular power. In terms of strength for weight, his vote was solidly for Perry, though he was quick to add that many other elements could intervene in an actual fight.

The Right to Fight

The one intervention that could be predicted with some confidence was from the police, themselves a recent innovation as far as the country authorities were concerned. Another was the use of the railway for transport to the fight. While it was not the first contest to make use of the new locomotion - Nick Ward had used it against Jem Bailey and Ben Caunt in the two previous years - it was probably the earliest to resort to what was destined to become the prize-rings favourite company, the Eastern Countries Railway. The special excursion train hired by fight organisers lay in the future, and the supposedly confidential arrangement was that all should embark on the scheduled 9.30 a.m. train to Sawbridgeworth, twenty-seven miles down the line. Unfortunately for those seeking to keep matters quiet, not only the circus-like trappings of the contest spread the enthusiasm more widely than usual, but also there were still fight followers tied to their travelling habits of the past. There was such a bevy of wagons and coachers on the road the night before that the authorities had clear warning of the general direction of events.

For all its many generations of avoiding the law, the ring had not yet accommodated itself to the existence of organized police forces in the countries. It was no longer just a case of avoiding a couple of magistrates, backed up by two or three part-time constables (calling out the yeomanry had been an exceptional event) as now even the shires were setting up their permanent uniformed forces, which they were empowered to do in 1839 and required to do from 1856. The early county forces were particular anxious to show that, even if they were not yet mandatory, they were efficient and necessary. Thus, when the heroes

29. Five Men in Blue Coats

of the day and their attendant host spilled from the train at Sawbridgeworth, there was the local superintendent of police, a magistrate at his shoulder, to greet them. Immune to such hindrances, though they had never happened before at a railway station, the leaders took the road towards the next county, Essex. The law intercepted them again. The superintendent was empowered to prevent them in Essex as well as in Hertfordshire. Where to now?

Cambridgeshire would have been a possibility but it was too far for the rail travellers, now reduced to the ranks of pedestrians. They would take that other frequent recourse and "try back", that is, return in the direction of the capital in the often fulfilled hope of finding somewhere quiet on the way. However, once the motley procession had apparently begun to beat the treat, the forces of law and order returned to their camp fires satisfied with their victory - and the fight began in the very field near Sawbridgeworth intended in the first place.

The Battle Begins

30. The Slasher and Freeman

By now thou, it was past 4 p.m. on a dull and darkening December day. Precisely at seven minutes after four o'clock the men were conducted to the scratch, their foggles having first been tied to their corner stakes, and having shaken hands with great good humour, the seconds retired to their corners. The towering height and gigantic proportions of Freeman led all to suppose that he would endeavour to fight down his opponent; but, as will be seen, this anticipation was not fulfilled. The Slasher stood on the defensive and Freeman broke ground hitting out with his left: from this the Slasher retreated, when Freeman followed him quickly, popped in his left and right. The Slasher again to the scratch, when Freeman led off left and right; the latter blow got well home, and dropped the Slasher. First knock down blow for Freeman; but no damage done, as the Slasher received it when retreating. The Slasher made play and tried his left on Freeman's body, but was stopped, Freeman rushed to him, the Slasher retiring and hitting short and wild. Freeman popped in his left and right, caught the Slasher in his arms, and threw him with ease. The Slasher on the defensive system, dodged a little, delivered his left on the ribs, in getting away he fell, and thus escaped Freeman's return. Freeman hit out left and right, but the Slasher ducked his head. The Slasher on the dodging system stepped back; Freeman after him to the corner, where there was a wild rally, in which hits right and left were exchanged. The Slasher got within Freeman's long arms, gave him a tidy smack with his right on the left eye (first blood from Freeman's brow, and the Tipton lads uproarious).

Foul or No Foul

The Slasher, the first to fight, hit out left and right, but was stopped. Freeman slashed away left and right but without precision. The Slasher popped his left on Freeman's ribs, and got away; Freeman after him, when the Slasher closed. Freeman lifted him clear off the ground, but was unable to get his arm loose, and after a short struggle the Slasher slipped from his grasp. The Slasher again led off with hits at the body, and in getting away fell from accident or design. (Cries of "foul" and "foul" were claimed on the part of Freeman; but the referee did not feel himself justified in stopping the fight, and "time" was called). The Slasher again tried the artful dodge, rushed into with his left at the body; but Freeman seized him in his powerful feelers, held him up for a short time, and finding he could do nothing at in - fighting fell on him, but not so as to do him any mischief. The Slasher as lively as ever popped in his left on

Freeman's arm and got away, Freeman followed, gave him one, two, left and right. The Slasher broke from him and delivered his right on his shoulder, then getting away, fell. The Slasher, once more led off with his left, but was short. Freeman after him delivered left and right.

Freeman popped in his left. The Slasher retreated. Freeman again planted his left slightly. The Slasher adhered to his retiring system. Freeman followed him to the ropes, and after a scrambling exchange of hits the Slasher got down. Freeman pointed at him derisively with his finger and laughed. Freeman hit left and right, and the Slasher rushed in and caught him around the body, to try for the fall; Freeman held him up completely off the ground by the neck, then chopped first with the left and then with the right; the Slasher hit up left and right, and caught Freeman on the mouth with his right; and after a short struggle was thrown. The Slasher again tried his left at the body, but was short, the blow falling slightly on Freeman's arm. Exchange of blows. Freeman with his left on the knob, the Slasher on his shoulder with his right, which sounded, but was of no effect. The Slasher came up on the defensive, but Freeman hit him down with his left. The Slasher again popped his left at the body. Freeman fell on him, and foul was claimed by Slasher's party, but not acknowledged, as it was obvious the fall was accidental.

The Slasher hit Freeman on the shoulder with his right, and in return caught it left and right as he retreated. Slasher returned to the charge with his right. A wild exchange of blows, but not effective, and the Slasher slipped down in retreating. (Twenty-three minutes had now elapsed, no real damage done on either side, and both as fresh as when they commenced.) The Slasher popped in his left on the body, and stepped back, Freeman after him, his left and right. Freeman delivered left and right; the Slasher was short in his return, and again received two pops left and right. Freeman delivered left and right. Freeman led off with his left. The Slasher popped in his left on the mark and tried to drop, but Freeman caught him around the neck and held him sometime, and then let him fall, tumbling over him, (another claim of foul not allowed). Freeman popped in his right on the Slasher's left eye. The Slasher countered on his shoulder, when Freeman caught him with his left. Freeman again planted his left, and, on Slasher rushing in, caught him in his arms, held him for a second or two, and fell on him. Freeman popped on his left, and dropped his man with his right. The Slasher hit short with his left, and renewed the dodging system, playing round his man. Freeman tried to nail him, but he got away, hit out with his left at the body, (another claim of foul for Freeman, not admitted).

The Slasher hit at the body with his left and broke away, Freeman after him, all for mischief, caught him on the hop. The Slasher delivered his right on Freeman's shoulder, broke away, and tried it with the left on the body, but was stopped. Freeman let go left and right, but the Slasher ducked and escaped. The Slasher again in with his left on the ribs and away; Freeman after him, caught him on the pimple. The Slasher hit short left and right, and was hit with Freeman's left. The Slasher pursued his left handed game at the body, but in getting away was hit with a touch from Freeman's left. The Slasher missed left and right.

(It now became so dark that it was difficult to see what was doing in the ring, and the spectators came closer to the ropes. The partisans of the Slasher were extremely uproarious, and one of them especially was consistently interfering with the umpires, called "time" when it was not time, and was guilty of other most offensive and unfair conduct). The Slasher, as usual led off with his left at the body but without effect. The Slasher hit short with his left, and was hit by a counter from Freeman's left as he was getting away. The Slasher planted his favourite body blow with the left, but without producing any visible effect, Freeman did not seem to feel it. Trifling exchanges with the left. The Slasher rushed in to make

31. Charles Freeman of Giant Girth

87

another effort for the throw, but Freeman again seized him in his powerful grasp, and fell with him, but not on him.

The Slasher down, but apparently no mischief done; and as far as the glimpse of light left would permit, we could discover no distinct mark of punishment on either man. The Slasher delivered his left at the body and fell, as if from the force of his own blow. Freeman fell over him, but evidently with no desire to avoid falling on him. (Another appeal was made to the referee on the ground of the Slasher falling without a blow, but the referee declared it was impossible to form a correct opinion, and expressed a strong wish that the fight should either be drawn or adjourned.) The Slasher down in each round, and Freeman avoiding falling on him. The Slasher in with his left on the body, but as he attempted to retreat Freeman caught him in his arms, held him for some time, occasionally chopping, and at last fell forward on him, with no consequence. The Slasher showed some fatigue, but came up full of confidence. He delivered his left at the body, but did not get well home, Freeman caught him left and right, and he went down to avoid further mementoes. To describe the remaining rounds would be an idle attempt in fact it became so dark that the men were only visible from the light colour of their skin and drawers. The Slasher pursued his dodging, and getting away, and falling system, occasionally making his left and right hits at the body and shoulder, and sometimes appearing to recoil from the effect of his own blows, but without producing any turn in his favour, Freeman hitting left and right, and now and then seizing his man, lifting him up, and flinging him down, but almost invariably avoiding falling on him, in one instance actually making an arch over his carcass, his head and legs on the ground, amidst the acclamations of the throng. In the last few rounds there was an evident attempt to draw Freeman into the Slasher's corner around which a desperate set of ruffians had collected.

Crowd and fighters miss train

The pugilists fought for nearly an hour and half, as the darkness and the fog closed in on them. The crowd broke the outer ring and swarmed round the ropes. The fighters became pale, shadowy figures, even from the ringside. Neither had suffered much damage and both were keen to reach a result, but the referee called a halt, saying that could see too little to be able to pronounce on any appeal made to him. The spectators were in such danger as the boxers had been when it came to finding their way back to the railway. In the unrelieved blackness, they stumbled into ditches, some fell into the canal, and many took hours to cover the short mile to the station. On arrival they found that all but the late train departed and that it did not arrive in London until midnight.

The Fight Continued (Tuesday 20th December)

The Slasher loomed large enveloped in a long white frieze coat, his head surmounted by an Indian fur cap, with a ferocious wildcat mask as a visor, which he wore upon his forehead. Ten Terry and Harry Broome were his benchmen. On stripping it was evident that Freeman had increased in bulk by a stone and a half – 18 stone 12lbs, being the result told by the weighing - chair that morning. His confidence too seemed to have increased in a corresponding degree. The Slasher, on stripping, looked thinner, and certainly paler than when he last peeled in Cambridgeshire, but he had lost none of careless "dare-devil" expression for which his countenance is remarkable.

At thirteen minutes after twelve precisely the men were conducted to the scratch, shook hands and threw themselves into position, the towering height and great bulk of Freeman presenting the same fearful odds we have before described. The Slasher dodged around his man, waiting for an opening, but he found the Giant ready to hit him, and he had already felt the weight of his feelers with sufficient force to have the prudence of keeping at a distance. The Slasher tried his left and right, but was out of distance. The Giant followed him in his pirouettes, and at last getting closer hit out left and right, the former passed over the Slasher's head, but the latter caught him slightly on the nut. The Slasher was again cautious. Freeman followed his dodging and at last rushed in to hit, but the Slasher in getting away fell without being struck, and got up laughing. The

Slasher got nearer to his man and let out with his left at the nob but did not get home. Trifling exchanges with the left, the Slasher retreating, Freeman at him left and right, just reaching him when the Slasher tumbled down. No mischief done. After renewed dodging the Slasher made himself up for mischief, feinted once or twice, and then hit out with his left. This brought the men to a rally, in which favours were exchanged, and the Slasher catching it on the nozzle showed first blood. After some wild fighting, hits were exchanged. Slasher cautious and getting away from the Giant, he at last steadied himself and counter hits with the left were exchanged. The Giant followed up his man to the corner, but missed both left and right. Counter hits with the left but no sting in them. The Giant hits out well with his right but the Slasher dodged and got away. The Slasher was short with his left and right, and again got away. He returned to the charge, and caught Freeman slightly on the body with his left. Freeman returned the compliment on the temple, but it was more of a shove than a blow. The Slasher hit short with his left, ducked and got away laughing. The Giant steadied himself waiting for the attack, stopped the Slasher's left, and caught him a stinger on the left ear with his right. The Slasher scrambled down in a sort of rally. The Slasher planted his right on the Giant's shoulder, and got away, the Giant after him.

Perry exchanges left and right, and flesh marks left. The Slasher pursued him, hitting widely left and right. He at last caught the Tipton in his arms and chopped him on the head several times with his right, but without administering any serious punishment. The Slasher tried his left, was short, and got away. The Giant followed him as he dodged around the ring, but his blows did not reach their destination. After a wild scrambling rally the Slasher got down. There was want of precision in Freeman's deliveries which forbade the hope of execution. The Slasher dropped a heavy smack on the Giant's ivories with his left, which, coming in contact with his teeth, inflicted a wound on his own finger that bled profusely. He tried it again, but was short, as was the Giant in his attempts to return. The Giant's mouth showed the effects of the blow in the last round, his lips were swollen a little, and a tinge of blood was perceptible. The Slasher led off left and right, the former on the ribs, and the latter on the shoulder, and rushing it after a struggle went down on his knees.

The Slasher came up laughing, the Giant looking serious, counter hits with the left. The Slasher dodged, and retreated towards the ropes, the Giant followed him and missed his own one two. The Slasher looked up, and laughed. The Slasher hit open handed, and retreated; he then tried to drop his left on the Giant dial, but his hand went over his shoulder; he then retreated, but finding the Giant rushing in for mischief, he dropped. (Cries of "foul" but the umpires did not interfere). The Slasher got home with his left, and dropped on the Giant's jaw. The Giant returned the compliment on the cheek, right and left. It scarcely could be called a knock down blow. The Slasher led off, and popped his left on the Giants mouth. The Giant after him and caught heavily with his right on the ear, which became seriously swollen. A rally, in which there were some heavy hits, exchanged.

The Slasher as usual, commenced hitting out left and right but did no execution, his blows being wide of their mark. Freeman to hit left and right but the deliveries were not affective. Freeman popped a heavy smack with his right on the Slasher's neck. The Slasher, stung, rushed in widely. The Giant steadied himself, hit out well with his left. The Slasher made play left and right, was short, and went down. His second was obviously rubbing his neck, and there was little of the doldrum appearance. The Slasher hit short and only reached Freeman's shoulder with his right. He then fought on the retreat to the corner. The Slasher showed symptoms of blowing. He led off in his old wild way, the Giant lunging out right and left, anyhow. The Slasher short with his left, and caught in heavily from the Giant's right on the ear, trifling exchanges. The Slasher again short in his deliveries. The Giant nailed him left and right, but not with much severity, then seized him in his arms and flung him down, walking contemptuously to his corner. Scrambling work. The injury to the Slasher left hand seemed to increase, but in this and the two following rounds no mischief was done. A wild blundering round, in which there was no precision on either side- the Slasher slipped down, but was up again and renewed the round. After a scrambling rally the Slasher again slipped completely under the Giant at who he looked up and grinned.

When to concede?

The Slasher hit short left and right and threw himself down with a whoop to avoid. Freeman laughed and shook his head, seeming to consider that it was intended to induce him to strike foul. The Slasher succeeded in planning a right handed chopper on the Giant's pimple and got away. The Giant dashed after him, hitting left and right, and then endeavoured to seize him, but the Slasher slipped away. Fighting wild and indecisive, in the last round, the Giant hit the Slasher down, but it struck us as rather a push than a blow. The Giant in the left and right- the Slasher retreated - the Giant after him, but it was no go - he let fly left and right, and then went down. The ground now became extremely slippy for both men. Freeman led off, but was short and wild, and did not reach his man. The Slasher popped his right on the Giant's shoulder. The Slasher rushed to close quarters, struck him on the shoulder with his right, but, on the Giant's attempt to return, he went down without a blow. A call was made by the seconds of Freeman's on the umpires, who disagreed, and upon appealing to the referee he pronounced "foul", and no doubt, had a similar appeal been made to him before he would have given a like decision. The Giant was immediately proclaimed the winner, and was taken out of the ring after fighting 39 minutes. The Slasher came up again "fresh as paint" and evidently but little injured by the contest. His left ear alone showed serious marks of punishment, it was much swollen and filled with coagulated blood. The finger of his left hand was likewise cut, but the contusions on his index were few and trifling consequences. He seemed anxious to renew the contest and denied he had fallen purposely. The judgement had been pronounced, however, and there was no recalling it. Johnny Broome was evidently mortified, and offered to put down a score for the Slasher to fight Ben Caunt, "there and then" Spring said such a proposition savored too much of passion and folly, but said Caunt was prepared to fight the Slasher or any man in England for one hundred to five hundred pounds, and the money was already at his house.

The Slasher always asserted that the decision was not fair and that he had slipped on the wet grass.

Remarks

This was an altogether unsatisfactory contest, the match was unequal, and the difference in the size of the men. Freeman already showed no lack of personal bravery, left no room for speculation on the issue. Everybody foresaw that the Giant must be triumphant, notwithstanding he fought badly. In fact he did not hit at points and missed most of his well intentioned but ill directed blows from the shifty character of his opponent, as well as from his own wild and uncertain mode of delivery. He hits around with his right, as the Slasher's ear testified, and his left handed deliveries are more like pokes than punishing hits. That he is a game man we have no doubt, but he is unwieldy, and possesses too much of "milk of human kindness" ever to become a "star" in the ring, even if his equal could be found. We are inclined to think, however, that this will have been his last appearance in the Prize Ring and should recommend choosing some more occupation - from his great size he will always be an object of curiosity. The Slasher is a mere rough who must be beaten by a well scienced man. That he would have shown to more advantage with a man of his own pretensions and size we have no doubt; but with Freeman he felt he could not cope to win, and therefore became reckless and careless- seeking only how to escape those visitations which, had he made "fair stand up fight" must have ended in more serious punishment. As it was, both escaped with comparatively trifling injuries, and remained to witness the subsequent fight. The Slasher's ear was reduced by a Surgeon who was on board the steamer. He was himself again, repeating that his going down without a blow was the effect of accident, and not design- assertion the truth of which few of who saw the performance were disposed to admit.

Although he had lost the fight, Perry had made himself a national reputation as the man who braved the American colossus for almost two hours and came out of it relatively unscathed. It might have not been either a polished performance or a dignified one, but at least he lived to tell the tale. He showed great hardiness, nimbleness and courage, though this "unknown novice" was still without any boxing skills apart from the craft and cunning from he had picked up from those around him to go down at will, to mock and taunt his

93

opponent, to drive him into his own corner, exposing him to the gibs and threats of the roughneck support he attracted these were, apparently the extent of the professional lesson which Perry had learned. He seemed unable to fend off Freeman's blow, while his own attacks where of the wildest, relying for the most part on a swinging right hand. Freeman, by contrast, was a revelation. He had quickly picked up some of the rudiments of orthodox boxing and but for the poor timing of his blows would soon have had his opponent floored. As it was, he always caught the Slasher on the retreat, never landing with full force; by never deliberately landing his own massive body on top of Perry's when he threw him. There was the same contrast in the behavior in the two men at the handing over of the stakes at Spring's Inn, The Castle. Freeman accepted his money with an impressive speech that was both fluent and modest, while the Slasher's responses to a few pounds raised by a collection for him was confined to rubbing the side of his nose and couple of grunts! His promoters, though, could see other pickings to be made, and Johnny Broome organized an extensive round of "benefits" and exhibitions, particularly in the industrial towns and cities, where the Slasher's somewhat basic talents had their strongest appeal. Freeman returned to the stage and the circus, only to die of lung disease within three years; Perry's party were quick to ascribe that to the battering he had received in their fight no matter what the medical evidence had said. Meanwhile, thought the motive for the Slasher's countrywide touring was strictly commercial, the constant sparring with the Broome's and preparation for the fight which was prevented by the imprisonment of his opponent served to improve the Slasher's technique. (the proposed encounter was against William Renwick of Liverpool, to be fought on Tyneside at £50 a side in August 1843, but Renwick was arrested at his training quarters a couple of days before the engagement). His new found skills took the opposition by surprise at his next encounter, against his second of former years, Tass Parker.

Friend or Foe?

Tass Parker has arrived in town, looking so "full of bloom" that he has been backed at 6 to 4, and even 2 to 1. He certainly is quite up to the mark, and books winning as a point already gained. The Tipton Slasher has been finishing his training at Stockbridge, under the watchful eye of Levi Eckersley, who pronounces him right well, and fit for the battle- field. The Slasher had hurt his right arm in setting – to with Harry Broome, at Bristol; but of this we have no personal knowledge, and learn that the blemish has been completely removed. Were it otherwise, we should scarcely anticipate that Johnny Broome, who says he has to find all the money, would have gone on with the match and he certainly speaks with great confidence. Parker has been visible at Owen Swift's every evening since Wednesday, and the Tipton Slasher will be at Johnny Broome's Air Street, Piccadilly, tomorrow evening. Tass Parker is most accomplished fighter none will doubt, but against him comes the rough and ready tact of the Slasher, who combines courage with superior weight. All we can hope is, that we shall have a fair and manly contest, and that the best man may win.

Suffice it, then, to say, that the voyage per steamer was safely carried out, and that the attendance of amateurs and professionals was immense, notwithstanding the severity of the weather and the dreary and inhospitable character of the Dartford Marshes, where the ring was pitched. Peter Crawley having consented to preside as referee, the performance began. In the opening rounds Parker displayed his superior skills, both in getting on to his man and getting away; but the Tipton and certainly greatly improved under the skilful mentorship of the Broomes, and was no longer the mere hardy rough which many yet considered him. He every now and then waited for, timed, and nearly stopped his clever and crafty assailant, inflicting severe punishment with his right upon Parker, who, finding he could not get near enough to deliver with exposing himself to heavy returns, soon began to fight shy. Indeed, round after round, after getting in a blow, Parker resorted to the reprehensible dropping system, not only to avoid hitting, but also to provoke and irritate his less skilful adversary and thus tempt him to deliver a foul blow, or, at the worst, to bring the fight to a "tie", "draw", or "wrangle". In this way sixty-seven rounds were fought, with no prospect of an approach to the decision of the battle. At this period- one hour and thirty – four minutes having been consumed the Kentish constabulary made their appearance, and stopped the tedious exhibition. The company, of necessity, re- embarked, and the disappointed excursionists returned to the Metropolis.

At a meeting of the men and their backers, at Peter Crawley's (the referee's), to arrange when and how their interrupted encounter should be concluded, Johnny Broome, on the part of the Tipton, asked a postponement for three months, and produced the following medical certificate.

"194, Blackfriars Road, Dec. 25th, 1843.

This certifies that we fused a fracture of the fore-arm of William Perry on or about the 7th November, and a fracture of the lower jaw on the evening of the 19th December. These serious injuries will require a period of at least three months before he can be a situation to fight again.

"CHARLES AND JOHN BRADY, Surgeons"

Parker, after some protestation against so long a delay, was met by Broome consenting to name that day ten weeks for the renewal of hostilities. Parker insisting on eight weeks, Broome consented to "split the difference", and, finally, that day nine weeks was agreed upon.

The adjourned battle was fixed for Tuesday, the 27th of February, 1844. Peter Crawley, who had been referee on the first occasion, declaring he had no further interest in the affair, left it to the parties themselves to settle their future proceedings. This was done by Jem Parker (Tass's brother), on the part of his Birmingham backers, and Johnny Broome, on behalf of the Slasher. It was decided to engage a special train on the Brighton line (an experiment which had proved successful on some recent occasions). The tickets at 10s. 6d. (about 50p) each, were secured under the guise of "an excursion"; the departure and return being arranged with the manager, so as not to interfere with the order and regularity of the traffic at the London Bridge terminus.

32. The Excited Mob of Noblemen, Gentlemen, Tradesmen and Pugilists

In consequence of the damage received by both men in their previous encounter, they were sent early into training, Tass Parker at Finchley, the Slasher near Tring, and, in point of condition, no two men could have been brought into better trim.

Shortly before one o'clock in readiness, the men were brought to the field, Tass Parker attended by Fuller and Tom Reidie, and the Slasher by Bob Castles and a Nottingham amateur. The former sported a flat of blue, with a white spot, and the latter a stone colour, with a pink spot. On entering the ring, they shook hands with apparent good humour, and each retired to his corner to prepare. Then came the important question - the selection of umpires and a referee. With respect to the former no difficulty was felt, and an amateur for the Slasher, and Jack Hannan for Parker, were named. The choice of the referee, however , was not so easily adjusted, and nearly an hour was wasted in discussing the merits of various persons named by both parties, each on his own especial behalf objecting to those offered by his opponent. On the part of Parker it seemed to be determined to have only one of four persons, and to five or six named by the Slasher, some of whom were persons of the highest respectability, a decided objection was made. In this way time progressively, but unprofitably, advanced, and the greatest impatience was displayed. At length Johnny Broome, on behalf of the Slasher, said he was willing that each should select a referee, and that those two persons should decide by toss who was to act.

The Fight Resumes

The men came up with their hands in good position, and after manoeuvring for a short time Parker let fly his left, which was cleverly stopped. This led to a rally, in which very trifling hits were exchanged left and right, but as they were out of distance no harm was done, with the exception of a slight discolouration on the Slasher's right cheek. Parker, in getting way from the Slasher's rush, fell on one knee. Parker again advanced bold as brass, looking all over confident, while the Slasher was not less prepared for action. After a few dodges, advancing and retreating, Parker popped in his left on the Slasher's cheek. The Slasher fought wildly left and right, missing some of his hits, but planting his right heavily on the ribs under Parker's left arm. Wild exchanges, when, as Parker was slipping on his knees, the Slasher caught his head under his arm, held it as if in a vice, and hung on him till he fell tumbling on him. The exchanges were trifling in their consequences, and a little flush on the skin was the only indication of punishment. Parker came up obviously undismayed by the result of the last struggle, and apparently resolved to do his best. He tried his left, which the Slasher neatly threw aside with his right. The Slasher then advanced, hitting left and right wildly, and Parker stepping back to avoid execution. Trifling exchanges with the left. Parker again away and watching for an opening to advance; dodging left and right, but no hitting. Parker stole a march, popped his left slightly on the Slasher's mouth and broke away, the Slasher wildly after him, hitting left and right, but Parker slipped down on his knees and evaded receiving thus commencing his old system. On the Slasher being picked up, blood was visible from his domino case, and this event was declared in favour of Parker. Parker again prepared to lead off, advancing and retreating finding the Slasher ready to hit or stop. At last he hit out with his left, which the Slasher stopped, and then rushing in left and right he administered a trifling upper cut with the latter, Parker retired to his corner, the Slasher after him. Parker in ducking to avoid, slipped on his knees, but was up again in an instant and popped in his left… The Slasher hit out left and right without precision, and after a wild, scrambling rally, without mischief, Parker slipped down. Slasher first up to the scratch, waiting for the attack. Parker dodged with his left once or twice, but not within distance. At length he got closer to his man, popped in his left on the Slasher's jaw, who countered slightly with the left, rushing after Parker who retreated to the corner; when he slipped down to avoid the Slasher dropping on his knees beside him. Parker afraid to approach his man. The Slasher hit out left and right, but was out of distance, and Parker broke away. Parker again dodging for an opening and on getting close up to the work, left-handed counters was exchanged, but the impressions were trifling. A wild rally, in which the Slasher got a slap on the mug, and Parker a heavy hit on the ribs from the Slasher's right. A scrambling exchange of hits left and right, when Parker slipped down. The hitting was wild, and anything but effective. The Slasher's mug somewhat flushed, but anything but serious in its aspect. Parker feinted with his left and popped in a pretty crack with his right on the Slasher's jaw, and then broke away. Dodging, but no hitting. The Slasher hit out left and right, but was short; Parker retreated to his corner; wild but ineffective exchanges left and right, and Parker dropped on his knees. Both at the scratch at the call of time. Parker tried his left, but was stopped; advancing and retreating. Parker endeavoured to steal a march, but was unable to get home, and the Slasher retired laughing. Parker again advanced, while the Slasher retreated; neither would go near enough to get to work. At last they got to a wild rally, missing their hits, and Parker retreating. Having reached Parker's corner, the Slasher weaved left and right, but did not plant his intended compliments. Parker slipped down, the Slasher upon him, Parker's right was puffered from the effect of one of his flying nobbers. Offers but no blows. The Slasher tried his right at Parker's nob, but was beautifully stopped, and Parker broke away. Parker advanced nearly to hit with his left, when the Slasher rushed wildly to him, weaving left and right, catching Parker on the left ear with the latter. In the scramble which followed Parker slipped down, the Slasher upon him. Parker's ear flushed, and his nose following suit in a slight degree. Parker advanced, but retreated the next moment, and the Slasher went to him. On getting to his corner there were slight exchanges with the left the Slasher hit over Parker's head with his right and Parker dropped. Parker slow to the scratch, and on the Slasher advancing he retreated to the ropes. A wild exchange of hits with the left, when Parker, again slipped down on his knees. No mischief done as yet, although Parker's flesh under the arm indicated the visitation to which it had been subject. Attempts left and right, in which both missed their blows. Parker broke away, slipped on one knee, but jumped up again. Wild exchanges, Slasher trying his left and right, Parker, ducking to avoid the Slasher, retreated, but again rushed to the charge, weaving left and right, ultimately slipping on his knees, amidst the cries of "cur". No sooner at the scratch that the Slasher advanced; Parker immediately retreated to the ropes, the Slasher after him; the Slasher hit out right and left, but Tass ducked under his arm, and escaped the intended compliments. Parker dropped on one knee, but again sprang up and caught the Slasher on the cheek with his left. Slasher missed his left and right, and Parker fell. Parker fought on the retreat: a wild scrambling rally to the corner, and the Slasher slipped down. Parker advanced and retreated, the Slasher after him, to his corner. Wild attempts at hitting left and right on the part of the Slasher, but he was out of distance, and missed. The Slasher then bored Parker down on the ropes, himself falling over outside the ring. Still no indications of serious mischief. The Slasher desirous of going to work, Parker retreating. The Slasher weaving left and right; an exchange of hits with the latter, and the Slasher again popped in his right on Parker's ear, from whence blood was visible.

Friends No More

The Slasher closed, forced Parker down on his knees, and fell on him. Parker on the retreat to his corner, the Slasher after him. Exchanges with the left and right, Parker getting prettily home with the former. A wild rally, both missing their blows, when Parker dropped. Slasher the first to the scratch, and full of fight; Parker retreated to his corner, the Slasher after him. Slasher hit out left and right, but without precision. Parker, on his guard, went down without attempting to hit. The Slasher, as usual, was the first to obey the call of time. Parker tried his left, but was cleverly stopped. The

Slasher then rattled to him;
Parker evidently ready to
drop, when the Slasher
slipped and fell. Parker
hugging his corner, when the
Slasher rattled to him, but
missed; wild hits left and
right. Parker popped in his
left and broke away. Slasher
again to the charge, followed
his man, caught him a heavy
whack with his right on the
jaw, from the effects of which
Parker staggered and fell. The
first knockdown for the
Slasher. Tass stopped, and the
Slasher rushed in wild left and
right. In the exchanges the

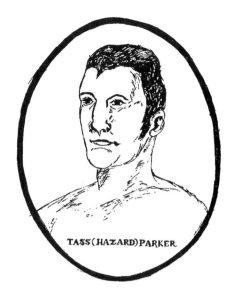

33. Tass Parker

Slasher had it on the mouth, but again planted his right on his shifty
opponent's pimple, when he got down. The Slasher the favourite and
offers to back him at evens. The Slasher first on his pins. Parker
retreated, the Tipton after him, hitting wildly left and right, Parker
dropped, but jumped up, hit out with his left, caught the Slasher
slightly, and again fell, amid exclamations of disgust. Parker slow
from his corner, the Slasher to him, when, after wild exchanges left
and right, with no execution. Tass went down. Parker came up
evidently a dastard in spirit, and upon the Slasher rushing to him he
slipped down, amidst the cries of "cur" and "coward!" Blood was
now flowing freely from the knuckle of Parker's left hand, which had
in some of the previous rounds come in contact with the Slasher's
tooth. From this to the thirtieth round Parker pursued the same
cowardly game of making a show as if he intended to fight, but the
moment the Slasher went to him to hit left and right purposely
dropping, and thereby avoiding the mischief which might be
affected. The Slasher was greatly incensed, turned round as if
appealing to the spectators, who shouted "cur" and "coward!" with
stentorian voices. The Slasher's umpire repeatedly cried "foul" and
nothing could have been more decidedly opposed to every rule of
fair play; but Hannah, Parker's umpire did not respond. He was

101

silent, but it was not difficult to discover which way his feelings inclined. In the thirtieth round Parker, after retreating to his corner, endeavoured to get down to avoid one of the Slasher's wild rushes. The Slasher endeavoured to hold him up, but in vain' down he went, and the Slasher dropped on him with his knees. Parker's backer immediately claimed "foul" amidst the derision of all around him. Parker went down fifty times at least, the Slasher most forbearingly avoiding all temptations to strike or even to fall on him so as to afford pretence of a claim of "foul". More than once Tass threw up his feet so as almost to kick at his man as he rolled or scrambled over him, after missing his one, two. It was in vain that the Slasher essayed to nail him left and right. He ducked and tumbled whenever there was the slightest chance of sustaining a hit, inducing universal marks of disgust at his cowardice, and the words "cur" and "coward" resounding from all quarters. In the fifty-seventh round the Slasher was lucky enough to afford him another excuse for a fall, by giving him a home slap from the left on the mouth, and laying him prostrate, while he pointed at him with derision. The real motive for refusing to agree to the appointment of an impartial referee now appeared to be in of no doubt. It had been foreseen that such a man would have long before this settled the point at issue by declaring the battle won over and over again by the Slasher. But even the absence of such a character did not serve the intended purpose. Hannan, who acted as umpire, declared his situation to be of a most unenviable description. He looked appealingly to all around him, and satisfied that the conduct of Parker was at variance with every principle of honour and fair play, he repeatedly sent to warn him that if he persisted in same atrocious cowardice he must agree with the repeated claims of his co-umpire, who in vain called for the honest and impartial judgement. The poor fellow actually trembled with vexation at the shouts of derision which were directed towards his man, and at length in the 120th round, on Parker going down without the most remote shadow of a blow, unless the wind of the Slasher's fist could deserve that character, he involuntarily exclaimed, in conjunction with his co-partner, and in accordance with the universal exclamations from every quarter of the ring "foul!"

Parker's Friends

This conduct on the part of Hannan elicited loud approbation, but in a moment he was surrounded by a knot of the most outrageous partisans of Parker, who threatened instant annihilation if he dared to repeat his just opinion. It was in vain we looked for the honest co-operation of the real members of the Ring to drive these ruffians from the arena. They ruled the roost without unblushing impudence, and threatened those who cried shame on their conduct with insolence and contempt. At last a second appeal was made to Hannan, but he was dumb, and nothing but a renewal of the fight would satisfy his assailants. Renewed though the disgraceful scene was, but with a perfect anticipation of what must be the ultimate result. Many gentlemen, old and sincere patrons of fair boxing matches, retired from the discreditable exhibition. The backer of Tass Parker asserted that he was so weak as to be incapable of keeping his legs, while every person who had the power of exercising the commonest judgement saw that when he thought proper he could stand as firmly on his pins as when he commenced. He had not, in fact, received a blow which could have, in the slightest degree, impaired his vigour, and were his heart in the right place, he was just as capable of continuing operations as the commencement of the fight. Hannan having resumed his seat, but pale as ashes, and shaking like a leaf, the farce was renewed, and for seven rounds more Parker got up but to fall in the same dastardly manner which had marked his career. In the 133rd round as he made a show of fighting, and exchanges left and right took place. Parker then retreated towards the ropes, the Slasher after him. When the Slasher was about to commence his wild and indecisive deliveries left and right, Parker finding he could not get away, for the last time dropped without a blow and the shouts "cur" and "coward!" were renewed with additional indignation. This was too much for Hannan, and incapable no longer of stultifying himself and the Ring of which he had been, and is, a gallant member, he at once agreed with the umpire on the other side that Parker had fallen without a blow, and had thereby lost the fight. Thus ended this libel on the "manly sports of the Ring". The roughs were taken by surprise, and were incapable of stemming the torrent of general indignation; but the weak and powerless Parker, in order to justify the false opinion expressed by his backer, jumped up with the vigour of a lion, and rushing to the corner where Johnny Broome stood, having possessed himself of the colours which had been tied round the stakes, tore his own colours from his hand, thereby proving that weakness was the least excuse which could be offered for his poltroonery. Everybody except the partisans of Parker was rejoiced at the termination of this most contemptible display, and heartily concurred in the propriety of Hannan's conduct.

The Third Contest Two Years Later

On the 4th of August, 1846 Parker for the third and last time entered the ring with "the Tipton" assuring his somewhat doubting friends that he had "screwed his courage to the sticking place" and determined to do or die. As the Slasher was now viewed by many as the "coming champion" the final contest between him and his scientific but soft-hearted opponent will be read with interest.

Lindrick Common, Nottinghamshire, eight miles from Sheffield, was the scene of action, the ropes and stakes being furnished by the Manchester Commissary. The attendance of the "upper crust" was by no means numerous, but there was a tidy sprinkling of Yorkshire sportsmen of the North-country Fancy, and a perfect crowd of swarthy miners and pitmen from the neighboring districts as far as Chesterfield and Derby. An excellent ring was formed, and, as the writer can testify, a degree of order observed which might well shame the "roughs" nearer home. At half past eleven o'clock the men entered the ring, Reid, of Sheffield, and Nobby Clarke waiting on the Slasher, Jem Parker and Cottrell, of Birmingham, seconding Tass. The betting was tolerably brisk at five to four on Parker, whose friends seemed to be in the ascendant, and certainly better "breeched" than those from "the Potteries". After nearly an hour's delay, owing to objections to several parties named as referee - the representative of Bells Life positively declining - Squire Edison accepted the office amidst acclamations, and the men faced each other.

The attitude of Parker, his left well up in a line with his left foot, and his right fore-arm slightly bent, and below the level of his left elbow, was graceful and attractive; he stood firm, yet springy, poised prepared for advance or retreat. His conditions appeared first- rate and his weight, 11st 6lb, seemed well distributed for activity and powerful effort; his countenance was smiling and confident and his age sat slightly upon him. His massive and ungainly antagonist offered a striking contrast; brown, burly, and "big for size" he grinned grotesquely as his slighter rival, nor was the oddity of his mirthful mug by any means lessened by the fact of his front railings having been displaced in bygone battles. He, too, was hard, and had evidently been brought, by severe training, into as good condition as we have ever seen him on former occasions. From the waist to the shoulders he was a model for a gladiator, but we doubt if the artist or the sculptor would feel inclined to copy his capital or his pedestals, while the latter more resembled the letter K than the parallel supports which society has agreed to term symmetrical. His weight was 13st 4lb; his age twenty-seven, having been born 1819, although the displacement of his grinders gave him a more antique aspect. Little time was lost in sparring, for the Slasher, his left presented and his right kept close to the mark, walked in upon his man, grinning mischief. Tass let go his left, but was stopped rather neatly; he broke ground and retreated, but the Slasher, working round forced him into his corner, where several sharp and rapid exchanges took place, Parker twice popping in his left, but effectively, and the Slasher countering, in one instance with a heavy hit on Tass's chest. After a little manoeuvring, the Tipton, resolved to force the fighting, stepped gradually in, Tass retreating and endeavouring to plant his favourite jab; it was a no go; taught by previous experience, the Tipton would not make play until his opponent let loose, and then, with more tact than we have hitherto seen him display, he countered with his left and bringing up his right caught Tass a sounder in the ribs. Tass leaped back, but renewed the hitting merrily, getting down at close quarters to avoid a return of the Tipton's right. Tass, serious, looked as if measuring his work; the Tipton grinning. Fast fighting for big "uns" seemed the order of the day. Tass got in on the Slasher's mouth. Who followed him fiercely, screwing himself up for mischief. Tass fought beautifully, but there seemed little sting in his deliveries; there was some excellent mutual stopping, which elicited applause, especially for the Slasher, of whom it was least expected. Tass again got in one on the Tipton's chest, who returned it with his right, and Tass went to earth. Parker again fought well. Merry work, but little harm done, till Tass sent his right, straight as an arrow, on the Tipton's left jaw, and down went his house, Parker also falling from his own blow. A uproarious first knockdown for Parker. Parker came up cautious, with an ugly cut over the right eyebrow. First blood for the Slasher. A short round; the Tipton again drove Tass before him to his corner, where he got down to avoid. As before, the Slasher seemed to have made up his mind there should be no idling; no sooner at the scratch than he was at work. Tass popped at him, but was short, and the Tipton missed his counter-hit. The Slasher laughed, and tried it again, but was stopped. A little rally at the ropes, and Parker, after an exchange or two, dropped on his knees. Tass manoeuvring, Tipton fighting, but not getting home. Tipton's seconds advised him to wait for Tass's play; he did so, and was rewarded by success. He met Parker, as he jumped in, with the left, and bringing up his right gave him a ribber that laid him on the earth, half doubled up. Slasher too fast, his opponent too slow. A short specimen of "You run away, and see if I don't come after you". At length Tass popped in a blow on Slasher's shoulder, who closed. A brief struggle followed; the Tipton got the crook with his crooked leg, and threw Tass. It was a boster (two to one on the Slasher). A short bout of hitting, stopping, and feinting. Tipton let fly, Slasher's left neatly stopped, and Parkers return parried. Parker flared up for a moment, and got in one, two, but produced no impression on his man, who went in laughing. Tass tried to evade him, but the Slasher closed; both down after a struggle, during which Tass's hand was seen across the Tipton man's face and a cry of "foul" was raised. Some confusion; Slasher appealed to the referee, charging Parker with the unmanly act of biting him in a previous round, when he was in, the act of throwing him, and in this round of an attempt to injure his eye. The referee ordered the men to proceed. Tass came up with a large black patch on his sinister eyebrow, and his most prominent feature somewhat damaged. Tipton eagerly after him, but Tass was too shifty to be immediately had; he gave the Slasher two pops; the latter. Tass held his arms almost at full extent, and manoeuvred, round his man; the Slasher, more cautious, faced him steadily. At length the men got nearer, exchanged blows, and Tass fell to finish the round. So soon as the Tipton went in, but Tass declined the compliment, and avoiding his one, two, fell to finish the round. Half a minute's posturing. Tass plunged in with his left, but was short; tried his right, but was stopped. The Slasher got close, Tass was unable to hit him off, and he delivered a half-arm prodder with his right. Tass fell because this time he could not help it. Tass played with his man; he seemed more than half tired of his job. The Tipton not to be drawn by feints. Slasher went in and down tumbled Tass. Parker came up slowly; good shops on both sides; Tipton, quitting the defensive, rattled in; Tass rallied sharply, but in the end received an ugly upper-cut on the dial, and fell. Tass somewhat disfigured, while the Tipton's ugly mug seemed altogether unaltered. After some slight exchanges Tass dropped. Parker's tactics seemed at fault; he sparred a few seconds, but on the Slasher stepping in, found his way to the ground rather equivocally. Tass flared up momentarily. He tried it on with both hands in succession. Tipton cleverly foiled him; Tipton returned. The old game was played- Tass selecting his mother earth. Tass's left again short; he was out of long blows. A close, and Tass got as well as he could. Parker made play, and getting a little nearer, dropped his bunch of fives on the Tipton's mouth, tried it again, but fell short, and got a left-handed nobber in return, that floored him neatly. Both Tass's hands seemed to have lost their cunning. His heart was not big enough to carry him in, nor, when thereby accident, to allow him to stand a rally. He fought badly and out of distance, and at length scrambled down to avoid the resolute chartre of the Slasher, who gave him a nasty one on the side of the nut as he was on his journey to earth. Perry drove his man all across the ring. Some pretty exchanges, Parker got home on Tipton's deal, who missed the return. A short, irregular rally. Tass again got in once or twice. At length the Slasher, who had been screwing himself up, sent out his left straight as an arrow at his opponents head. The concussion was like the kick of a coach horse, took effect at the base of Parker's left nostril, and he fell as if shot. "It's all over" was the cry; and the Tipton remained for sometime in the middle of the ring to favour the company with a few polka steps, for which his swing leg was peculiarly adapt. And last- Tass, to the astonishment of all, came up at the call of time, but it was evident the last hit been a settler and had sent his faculties all abroad. Although he assumed an attitude, he stirred perplexedly at his opponent, and swerved from the perpendicular as he broke ground. The Tipton surveyed him a moment before he stepped forward, but no sooner did Tass perceive his approach, than, either from bewilderment or a feint heart, he fell forward on both knees, and hence on his hands. The Slasher turned appealingly to the umpires and referee, without having offered to strike. The case was clear; and amid the shouts of the multitude the Slasher was greeted as the conqueror. Time, twenty seven minutes.

Remarks

The Slasher fought better than we have seen him on any previous occasions; his confidence and conditions - of which later absorbed rumours were afloat - were on par with his coolness and courage. To the former he had tact in waiting for his opponents delivery of a blow, and a skill in counter-hitting for which we did not give him credit; this added to his physical superiority in weight, left his lighter and more active opponents almost without a chance, and the contest was reduced to a mere question of time, the ultimate result being scarcely with the scope of doubt. Of the defeated man we can only say that although he fought three or four rounds in a spirited way, an almost desperate manner, his conduct in the vast majority so much savoured of Falstaff's "better part of valour" that his claim to the character of a game man still remains unproven, while his attribute of skill, so loudly vaunted by his infatuated admirers, as suffered considerably by this exhibition; this, however, may partly be owing to the improvement in his antagonists tactics which, by frustrating his early efforts, so disheartened him, that he never showed to less advantage. The question of superiority can no longer be muted; Tass's quickness and skill have lost their striking advantage, while the Slasher's strength and pluck, on this occasion seconded by the a respectable amount of science, have by no means fallen off. Tass's friends attribute his defeat to his having had two ribs broken in the seventh round, from the Slasher falling heavily on him, and he certainly remained under the surgeons hands, who confirmed the aforesaid fracture.

The Other William Perry

The other William Perry appeared at the end of 1845, introduced by Caunt. A Negro described as "formidable" standing over six feet and weighing 13 stone. This mysterious man displayed such talent with the fists, when he beat Bill Burton of Leicester in January 1846. This was the first and the last appearance of the so called William Perry in the English prize ring. He proved to be connected with a gang of forgers of American bank notes, being previously imprisoned more than once. He was transported to the Antipodes.

In 1849 the Yankees were boasting of a new champion named Hyers who had beaten everybody on his own Continent and in consequence defiance was sent over to England. The Slasher was regarded as the most formidable man in England at that time and was invited to the United States, Hyers offered to pay his expenses across and to fight him for any sum.

Bendigo's challenge or lack of it

Several fighters challenged the Slasher between the years 1846 to 1849 but all forfeited making the Slasher substantially richer. During this period in his life he became a wealthy man through exhibitions and benefits of the Noble Art.

The year 1850 saw William Perry aspire to claim the title Champion of England. Bendigo refused to hand over the Champion Belt and Perry through Bell's Life requested according to agreement he hand the Belt over or Tipton would offer the chance of Bendigo retaining the Belt by making a match with his goodself.

Bendigo's only challenge to the Slasher was through a poem.

"Bendigo, eighty rounds were fought
when Caunt he could not rise
and all declared the bendy cock had fairly now the prize
the Tipton Slasher now may come but soon he'll get to know
that he was not quite big enough to wallop Bendigo."

Sport writers of the time made no secret of the fact that Bendigo did not fancy the job, bold Bendigo was as clear with his tongue as with his fists. Bendigo Caunt and Deaf Burke both side-stepped the Slasher, Bendigo never returned the belt.

Caunt Backs Down

After the battle, the Tipton Slasher issued a challenge to Caunt to fight for £100 a side; this Caunt declined to do, and staked £500 in the hands of the editor of Bell's Life, declaring, at the same time, his willingness to fight the Slasher for £500, and for no smaller sum. Much angry correspondence passed between them, which is utterly unworthy of preservation; and in the latter part of 1846 Johnny Broome presented a belt to the Slasher, whereupon Caunt lowered his terms to

34. Ben Caunt

£200, with a stipulation that if the condition was not accepted within a month, his retirement from the ring was absolute. This, however, was not suitable to Broome & Co., though the Slasher was ready and willing. The Slasher was keen now to show his worth against the best. But it did not suit Johnny Broome's book and it was Johnny, through his rich clientele at the Rising Sun held Perry by the purse strings. He had his eye already on another up and coming lad from the West Midlands, Tom Paddock. It was, indeed, a bad time for someone of the Slasher's position, on the very brink of the Championship. The five years between 1845 -1850 were notable for the absence of fights between the big men. Deaf Burke had died in 1845, aged 35, having regarded himself as being in contention almost to the end. Bendigo had his tenacious hold on the title and was reluctant to put it at risk. Neither he or Ben Caunt had very

34A. Local artist's illustration of The Champion, Spon Lane, West Bromwich taken from the only known existing photograph circa 1857.

strong motives for fighting - both were in their 30s and there were easier picking from tours and exhibitions. The stakes that might have tempted them were just not forthcoming, with interest from the moneyed classes at its lowest ebb. Recent fights had hardly justified anything else. Too many of them had been mere parodies of what the old school expected from the traditional "fair, stand up fight". Most were neither. The increasing problems of evading both the police who saw to prevent fights and roughs who sort to disrupt them were strong deterrents to the widening range of the population that it saw itself as respectable and law abiding. Only Tom Paddock was active, fighting his way up to title contention himself, as another of Broome's "unknown novices". The Slasher could do little but sit on the side lines during these years when he was in his prime. His frame, never puny, had filed out impressively. Topping six feet, he usually had the advantage of size and weight over his opponent. There were no more Freeman-like giants. Years of wielding the shovel had built up his shoulders and biceps. And, from the waist upwards, he was a fine figure of a heavy-weight. The slightly crooked leg spoiled the symmetry of his appearance, but it was of little practical hindrance in the ring. His rough features, creased early in life so that he always looked older than his years. Because all the more fearsome, as the number of gaps in his teeth grew for all his threatening demeanour, he remained a rough and relatively naïve Black Country Lad, more receptive to lessons in the dodges of the Prize Ring to learning its more subtle skills. Parrying blows, weighting and counter punching never became ingrained boxing habits with him, and the old primitive Slasher was always likely to emerge, but he was beginning to learn and to learn more than just ringcraft. He was firmly rooted in his native Tipton. His own tavern was called "The Champion" (of England), in Spon Lane, West Bromwich. He was a familiar figure at the many local prize fights, making the early acquaintance of Tom Paddock when he seconded "Nobby" Clarke against him at Coleshill in 1846. But these fallow years did not suit him. Being a local hero had its small glories, and he was always assured of a vociferous following, but he had the ambition for much more. He was ready to break away from the Broomes, who had shackled his fighting career as much as they promoted it.

Even when the chance of the fight did come up, in 1849, the Slasher's ill luck continued to dog him. He had to forfeit on accounts of illness, to Con Parker, another brother of his old opponent, who he would, to judge from their records, have beaten convincingly. His next chance of fight, with the thriving Tom Paddock, was apparently scotched by his own backers, who managed to contrive a "draw" with Paddock's people and secure the return of the stakes. However, this proved to be only a delay. The Slasher broke free from his old associates when new backers appeared. The articles for the Paddock fight were revived and Perry found himself in new company. He moved to Liverpool to train under Levi Eckersley, with Jem Ward in the background, and Tom Springs at the Castle became his London base. Under these veterans he was able to breathe in the last few gasps of the old classical pugilistic world.

The fight with Paddock was an eerie affair in the moonlight and the almost obligatory ending with Paddock striking a violent foul blow after a round was ended. At least for the Slasher the encounter was a satisfactory one. He was healthy, fit and strong, and he used his power and experience to demonstrate to young Paddock that the rushing tactics he had used against the light and aging Bendigo of were of no avail here. Paddock was terribly punished about the face, putting the eventual

35. Tom Paddock

winner beyond doubt, foul or no foul. The land of promise thus reached, the office was given, for the last time, to disembark. A side for a ring was quickly discovered, and although not a very desirable spot, still, it was the only one to be had, and no time was lost in forming the magic square. A limited outer-ring was also formed, the

113

tickets, at 5s. each, distributed to those who sought the privilege of a close proximity to the scene of the action, the produce being afterwards equally divided among the ring keepers. It was now 4 o'clock, and the day fast waning; in fact, it was difficult to distinguish the faces of persons from one side of the ring to the other; but a clear moon hung out its lamp, and promised a continuance of light. All being in readiness, Paddock flung his castor into the ring, following it himself amidst loud cheers. He was attended by Jack Hannan and Bob Fuller. The Slasher, who was not long after, was waited on by Nobby Clarke and Jem Molyneux. Paddock looked fresh, laughing, and apparently confident; while the Slasher was cool, quite and smiling, after a great deal of difficulty as to the selection of referee, both parties agreed upon Ned Donnelly. Jem Burn addressed this functionary on the part of Paddock, and said all he wanted was a fair and manly fight, and that there should be no objections to any accidental occurrence. He wished the merits of the men might be fairly tested, and only desired that the best man might win. The men now prepared for action, and at 30 minutes past 4, the rising moon looked modest from the East, and the last rays of the setting sun painted the western horizon, the gladiators appeared at the scratch, and commenced.

The Fight

The men having chosen their corners, fortune enabled the Slasher to place his back to the rising moon, so that his tooth-less mug was in shade. His Herculean frame was, however, sufficiently visible, and his easy confidence and quite deportment increased the confidence and of his friends, and led all who scanned his proportions to consider him perfectly competent to hit down a hippopotamus; or, like the Greek boxer of old, floor a cantankerous bull. Paddock, although when opposed to Bendigo he appeared of the burly breed, loomed small in contrast with the Slasher. The disparity in their size was obvious, and as he jumped about seeing an opening, a veteran ring-goer exclaimed, "It's any odds against the young' un, he's got his master before him now". In fact the very style of holding up his hands, and the yokel-like feints (completely out of distance) with which he commenced, showed he was puzzled how to begin the job

114

he had so confidently undertaken; presently he determined to chance it and jumped. Fortune favours the bold, and he gave the Slasher a clout on the jaw-bone with his left, the Tipton hitting in return on his shoulder or breast, and driving him back. The Slasher stepped in; Paddock retreated before him to his corner, hitting up again, but the Tipton stopped him. A smart exchange took place, and Paddock slipped down to get out of mischief. Paddock began by trying his left twice, and barely reaching the Slasher who dealt him a body blow with the right. Some heavy hits in weaving style, a half round body blow or two followed the sound rather than the effect of the hitting being perceptible. The Tipton closed with Paddock, who struggled for a moment, and was then thrown on his back, the Tipton lending him thirteen stone additional to hasten fall. 2 to 1 on the Tipton. The Slasher missed Paddock two or three times, owing to his active, jumping away; still he steadily pursued him. Paddock tried both hands, but had the worst of the exchanges; still there was no harm done. Paddock made a lunge with the right, but Tipton met him a smasher, and hit him down, almost falling over him. First knock-down for the Slasher. It was now stated that Paddock had dislocated his shoulder; it was no doubt injured, but not out of joint. He tried his left in a flurried manner, but the Tipton feinted with the left, drove him back and Paddock fell to avoid. The Tipton went to work quickly, but steadily; he caught Paddock on the body with the right, and on the left cheek heavily with the left, as he was jumping round. And down went Paddock among the bottles in his own corner. Tipton gave Paddock no rest or time for reflection, but pelted away. Paddock skipped about, and escaped against the ropes; from his corner, hit up, catching the Tipton on the side of the neck slightly, and dropped on the knee. The Tipton might have given him a finisher, but did not avail himself of the chance, threw up his hands and walked away. Paddock hit Tipton sharply with the left on the forehead as he came in. Tipton missed his right but caught Paddock a nasty blow on the nob as he was going back. Paddock fell on the ropes but was not down. The Tipton dropped his hands and came away from him, disdaining to hit him in that position. "Bravo, Tipton!" As before; making the play and forcing his man, he could not make head against the attack, and jumped about like "a parched pea". Paddock fell at Tipton's feet, who, the friends of Paddock declared, tried to tread on him, and appealed accordingly. It was a "forlorn hope", and the referee said "he saw nothing foul". Paddock jumped up as usual, just reaching Tipton's chin, for which he was punished with a sounding ribber. Exchanges, but no effect visible, except a little blood for Paddock's cheek. First blood for Tipton. The Tipton hits out right and left, and caught the Redditch man on the nob and body, who staggered half-way across the ring, and fell. Tipton once again on Paddock's body. Paddock fell in bustle without a hit. Paddock shifting and retreating. A slight exchange, and Paddock fell to avoid. Tipton forced Paddock into his corner, but before he could do any mischief Paddock fell. A claim of "foul" but not acknowledged. Tipton just touched Paddock with his left, who kept slipping back. Tipton followed him and he dropped. Another appeal that Paddock fell without a blow, but the Tipton party waived the objection. Paddock hit Tipton then slipped half down, jumped up again, and resumed the fight. Tipton went to work, and hit him down in the short rally. Slasher made at Paddock who wouldn't stand his charge, and fell to avoid. Appeals "We don't want to win by foul", said the Tiptonians. Paddock's right arm hung as if disabled, but he brought it into play when action commenced. The Tipton drove him to the ropes and hit him down. Paddock, in jumping away, caught his right heel against the centre stake, and stumbled down, but jumped up again. Seeing Tipton close on him, however, he dropped on his knees. As the moon got higher, the light improved. The Tipton, in bustling Paddock, got a body hit which he reported with a heavy- hander on Paddock's smelling organ, and down he went quite bothered. Paddock came up with face painted carmine colour, and was no sooner at the scratch than he was down. Another appeal. Wild exchanges. Paddock on the shift. The Tipton gave Paddock, a topper on the head, high up, when he fell, and Tipton over him. A slight rally in Paddock's corner. Paddock rushed at Tipton, who made an awkward step back. Paddock pushed rather than hit him with the left, and forced the Tipton over, (Cheers for Paddock). Tipton went in with both hands, and Paddock fell without a blow. Appeal repeated. And last- the odds were the Great Glass-case of 51 against a cucumber-frame.

"Never Turn Your Back"

The Tipton gave Master Paddock a pelt on the head, and began punching. Paddock dropped, and the Tipton was about to return to his own corner, as he had several times done, when up jumped the Redditch man, and rushing at the Slasher, lent him such a dig just at the back of the left ear, with his right, that down tumbled Tipton, half with astonishment, half with the blow. And as Paddy would say "the third half of him fell just because it was not used to stand upright". A more palpable "foul" was never seen. The spectators jumped from their seats, and all sorts of people got into the ring. The Tipton walked towards the referee for his decision, and that functionary pronounced it "foul"; "and so ended the great little fight for the Championship, in forty-two minutes, the dial showing twelve minutes after five.

And this exhibition was certainly a complete "pig-shearing" excursion. The Slasher was not only in splendid condition, but his method of fighting, long arms, and great experience, made it no match. True, he was not to blame that it was so bad a fight, for as one man can take a horse to water, but twenty can't make him drink. As to Paddock, he was so manifestly over-matched, and over-rated, that he had not the shadow of a chance; and the rush that proved perilous to Bendigo- old, stale, under 12 stone, and a practice of retreating tactics-was not only useless against the bulky, firm-standing Slasher, but was certain destruction to the assailant, from the Tipton's tact at countering his superior strength, and immense weight. In fact, it was "a horse to a hen" on all points.

The return to the carriages was as speedy as circumstances and awkward clayey drains and ditches would permit, but all were safely seated, the agreeable whistle of departure sounded, and the whole party delivered at the Nine Elms terminus by six o'clock; the Slasher, merry as a gig, and loudly cheered, while Paddock complained on severe injury to his shoulder, which, if serious, was certainly aggravated by his last effort to do unlawful execution. The Tipton was received at the "Castle" with a flourish of "See the conquering hero comes!" while Paddock quietly returned to the "Queen's Head", where he received surgical attendance; and it was officially reported that he "had injured the bone of his shoulder, and that a sling must be worn as a safeguard against the consequences of moving the joint".

The Dudley Devil – Who was he?

Theophilus Dunn was said to have a contract with "The Black'un". His neighbours described him as a wizard, but such was his fame that his clients travelled many a mile to see him and seek consultation. These days we may scoff at such claims but Dunn flourished at a time in an area that still believed in witchcraft.

36. The Dudley Devil
An illustration by Dorothy Beauchamp

Pedalling his charms for all ailments known to man at a shilling (5p) a time, the Dudley Devil claimed to be able to see into the future and a prophecy (the one that he gave to the Slasher) went in to Black Country folklore.

Hickman, a local bare-knuckle boxer, visited Dunn's Fortune Telling Booth at one of the many Black Country wakes. He mocked at the prophecy that he would die at an early age crushed by coal. Hickman, who had never been in a coal pit in his life, poured scorn on the claim. However his untimely end was not far away. Intoxicated, he drove his horses in an attempt to overtake a fully laden coal cart and in so doing overturned his own cart and was thrown to the ground. The wheel of the coal cart passed over his head crushing it like the "Devil" had forecast. The Dudley Devil's fortune was thus made and he lived well on the proceeds of his profession.

The Fall

In the early 1850s the Slasher went to the Dudley Devil's to have his future told. Dunn, was an astute psychologist, and if any person could foretell the future he could, for he was right too often for the laws of probability. He was not a philanthropist and forecast only when his palm was substantially crossed with silver. He would word his prophecies in a rude alliterative rhyme similar to Nostradamus, although he had probably never heard of him.

To the Slasher he said:

"Slasher, yoh'll stop as yoh started,
Yoh'll get all yoh gi'ed in one goo;
Yoh and yer pub will be parted,
Tom Little will mek it cum true".

Like the rhymes of Nostradamus, the truth of this was not patent until after the event. The Slasher was retired and did not intend to fight again. There was no mortgage on his pub and he had plenty in the bank. In any case, who was Tom Little? The person of little Tom Sayers, was just making his name in the Prize Ring - and in 1857 he was to make every word of the rhyme come true.

Perry was at the peak of his career. He once again made a loud claim to the championship. When Bendigo would not take up a specific challenge - at 40, he at last admitted that his fistic days were over - Perry threw the challenge open to all for £100 or £200 at will. The answer eventually came from a surprising quarter. Johnny Broome put forward yet another of his "unknown's"

37. Harry Broome

who turned out to be none other than the Slasher's old sparring
partner from the touring days, Broome's younger brother Harry. The
Slasher completed another provincial tour before going into training
again with Jem Ward, while at the London end young Spring had to
take over from his dying father. For a championship fight it aroused
little interest in the capital and scarcely 100 passengers turned up to
catch the special train, the only representatives of the old school
being Tom Oliver and Peter Crawley. The latter at length agreed
upon as referee - with some reluctance on the part of Perry because
it was felt (without justification) that he was likely to favour the
Broomes. It was a much harder fight that the Slasher had expected
from his knowledge of Harry. The skills were expected, but not the
confidence and aggression, and especially not the strength of his
wrestling which repeatedly had the heavier man on the turf. Matters
stood about equal when the usual unsatisfactory ending came about.
The Slasher landed a blow as Broome fell to the ground.

Peter Crawley, looking nothing like 'Young Rump Steak' of former times,'take. off his jacket' to The Slasher......

38. Peter Crawley

Impartial observers agreed that it was foul but accepted that it was a
mistake and unintentional, doubting whether it could have been
brought back once Broome started to go down. The Slasher's

120

supporters were furious, vociferous and violent. He himself was in a high temper and accused Peter Crawley of bias. The sight of the venerable and portly Peter struggling out of his coat to take on Perry himself to answer for the insult to his honour brought some bitter humour back to the scene and Perry was ushered away still loudly proclaiming himself to be the champion.

Harry Broome, prematurely overweight, retired to his victualling interests and Perry's claim had validity.

39. Harry Broome Felled

Certainly, no one sought to face him, and he repeated generous dominations by way of lost deposits when fighters or their backers, had second thoughts - £25 from Harry Broome when the rematch fell through, £70 from Aaron Jones in July 1856 and £80 from Tom Paddock a few months later. Perry, who had been twenty-one years before the public, now became a publican.

The New Belt

A subscription was made by the leaders of the Fistic Art for a new belt, which was of a greater value than any that previously existed. This was done as an inducement for some of the heavyweights to throw down the gauntlet and rescue the declining sport. A sum of £100 was collected and as the other belt had gone astray, terms were drawn up.

Rules:

The Belt should not be handed over to any person until he has proved the right by a fight. Any pugilist having held it against all comers for three years without defeat should become the absolute possessor.

Described As The Old Philistine

"Man Of Might"

A dinner at Nat Langhams was given to celebrate the victory of Little Wonder over Aaron Jones. A discussion between Bill Hayes and Jemmy Massey, the latter was a great friend of Old Tipton, sang his praises, declaring there was no other man capable of holding a candle to him. John Gideon differed, saying the Slasher was old and stale. It was stated that as they all were acquainted and aware that Mr. William Perry had during these few years been taking little care of himself. He gave a description of William as being "a rackety sort of fellow". When he became licensee of the Champion of England, Spon Lane, West Bromwich, he lived an exceedingly unsteady life. The business he did was very good for he acted as a purveyor of refreshments at many Midland race meetings and became very popular in the Black Country.

The first signs of decline, though, had been there in the fight with Broome. Some of the agility had gone and the swinging blows did not come with quite the same speed and power. The continued waning of Perry's abilities was finally and clinically exposed by Tom Sayers on 16th June 1857, and the Slasher's reign troubled, intermittent and seldom certain, was at last over.

Six years had elapsed when "the Old Tipton", as he was now popularly designated was dared to the field by this new David. Right cheerfully did the old "Philistine man of might" – for the Tipton never lacked personal courage- respond to the "little uns" crow. How the oft- repeated error of "trusting the issue of battle to waning age", was again exemplified on the 16th June, 1857, at the Isle of Grain, when the once formidable Slasher was conquered in the contest for £400 and the Champions belt by the marvelous little miller, Tom Sayers. This was the closing scene of the Tipton's long and chequered career. He retired, defeated but not dishonoured, to his native town and early associates. In his latter days the Tipton is said to have never refused "a drink for the good of the house".

At the side of the first canal in Spon Lane, opposite to the Cape Hotel, stood a house which was once licensed under the name of The George Inn. It is of undistinguished appearance and its only claim to fame is that for seven years it was home to the Slasher. The name of the landlord boldly painted above the door, William Perry - Champion of England known locally as "Perry's Pump". The pub was described as a seedy place, smoke encrusted on the outside and mean within, a temple of splendor. The unconquered, the undisputed chieftain of the fighting clan, he reigned there for years, none daring to make him afraid.

While at the George Inn, he gave lessons in boxing to some of the young bloods of the district and the house became the resort of the local leaders of the Pugilistic Fraternity in Spon Lane.

The year 1856 saw the number of Inns or Taverns in Spon Lane as seven while the Beer Houses totalled twenty-three. A Beer House sold only beer as its name implies and it was seen as an escape for pugilists who had no other profession than fighting. A licence was granted for £2 enabling homes to be turned into licensed premises giving a source of income and a chance to earn a reasonable living.

The Parish of Tipton in 1834 with its large influx of people possessed thirty taverns and sixty Beer Houses. The Beer House went out of fashion in the 1900s when a total of 150 public houses served the Parish thirst which was once described as "unquenchable".

At what period of his career Tom first became inspired with an ambition to win the Champion's Belt I am unable to say, but I have no doubt that he had secretly cherished the notion long before he let any human being know the dearest wish of his heart. Having proved in his victories over Harry Paulson and Aaron Jones that he feared no odds of height and weight, and that it was all the same to him whether his opponents were ten stone or twelve stone, "Tom felt that the time had come when he might reveal to the public his long-cherished desire to try for the highest trophy the Prize Ring had to bestow." To Sayers himself there was nothing ridiculous in his ambition. But, after his second victory over Aaron Jones, he formally challenged the renowned Tipton Slasher.

Everybody said it was a ridiculous match. When I say everybody "I mean of course, the people who thought they were "everybody", and were confident that anyone who did not agree with them was a fool. In this case, however I am bound to say that "everyone" included opponents of the sporting public who took an interest in the Prize Ring. You see, it was such an utter reversal of mad revolutionary idea to match a 10st 10lb man of 5ft 8 ½" in against a 14 stunner of over 6 ft., and the latter, mind you, "no" duffer, but the Champion of England, who had won his title by hard fighting. For till then it had been a recognized fact that no man who did not come above the heavyweight limit -12st - had any right to fight for the Belt and would not even find a backer.

Slasher had fought ten big battles, and had licked Barney Dogherty, Ben Spilsbury, Jem Scunner, Tass Parker, (three times) and Tom Paddock. He had been beaten after a draw by Freeman, the American giant, who stood 6ft 10 ½", and weighed 18st. in condition. The two fights with Freeman were farcical. The Slasher was so awed by the tremendous height and reach of his opponent, who was as active as he was powerful, and a splendidly made athlete to boot, that he did not attempt to face him in fair stand-up fighting. If he had gone resolutely at the giant I am inclined to think he would have licked him, for Freeman was a bit soft, and if tackled at close quarters, would not have held out long. Harry Broome, he won his fight with the Slasher on a foul – the big "un" hit his man when he was down on his knees; not intentionally, but simply from the fact that, having launched his blow when Harry was falling, he could not check it. But it lost him the fight, though in any case Broome must have won if his wind had held out, for he proved himself to be a better wrestler and a better fighter than Slasher. The Tipton's best fight was with Tom Paddock. He used his long reach with great effect. One thought how easily he kept Paddock at arm's length and how he stood like a rock against all Tom's furious rushes, hitting him back with consummate ease whenever he came in. It was difficult to see what chance Sayers, a much lighter and shorter man than Paddock, could have against the mighty Slasher.

It was after this fight with Paddock that the Tipton claimed the Championship, as Bendigo declined fighting again. He lost the title when Harry Broome beat him; but, as Harry forfeited to him in a second match, and then retired from the Ring, the Slasher again claimed the title.

The Fall From Grace – Tom Sayers -V- William Perry

When, at last, the two heroes of the hour, each attended by his seconds and bottle-holder, carrying carpet bags appeared at the ring-side, there were loud cheers as they flung caps into the "magic circle". They had just tossed for corners, and were about to commence the contest, when there was a cry of "The Bobbies! Look sharp on board!" It was no false alarm, for five men in blue coats, white trousers and glazed hats which then formed the uniform of the "peelers" appeared upon the rising ground and were seen making

40. All running for their lives towards the river

125

straight for the ring. No words can adequately describe the skedaddle "which followed- three thousand people, old and young stout and thin, smells and toughs, all running and tumbling over one another in their frantic haste, rolling into ditches.

The Ring Reset

In a very short space of time there must have been fully three thousand people gathered round the ring, which Oliver had again set up. The roofs of the aforesaid sheds were black with rows upon rows of spectators, who had a splendid and uninterrupted view of the arena. The ring had been pitched upon a far more elevated site than before, and so great was the rush of swells for the privileged enclosure, that more than £50 was realized by the sale of inner-ring tickets. It was just half past four when for the second time for combatants entered the lists. Both men had as their seconds former antagonists, for Nat Langham (Tom's only conqueror), assisted by Bill Hayes, waited upon Sayers, and Tass Parker with Jack MacDonald on the Slasher. The latter pair were the best seconds living at that time, and anyone who knew how much clever seconding has to do with the winning of a fight augured well for the Tipton's chances with such able henchmen to tend him.

Never since Tom Johnson fought the gigantic and Herculean Isaac Perrins for the championship in 1789 had two men so utterly ill matched in size been seen in the Prize Ring. The Slasher looked immense. He stood 6ft 1in, and scaled drawn, 14st 2lb. but the mere statement of his height and weight can convey no idea of the colossal proportions. I have never seen a broader man or one with such huge shoulder blades. There wasn't an ounce of superfluous flesh on him anywhere. His great gaunt, bony, powerful frame, his long muscular arms, his massive hips and thighs seemed to hold strength enough to defy half a dozen such pigmies as Sayers. His attitude, indeed, was ungainly, owing to a deformity of one of his legs, which was "K" shaped, but those who had seen him fight knew well with what wonderful quickness and agility he could turn and wheel pivot- like on that crooked pin. When he smiled the effort was ghastly, for all his upper front teeth had been knocked out, and you

126

could see plainly on his brown, tightly-drawn skin the white seams and scars that told of grisly wounds in many a hard- fought fray. He looked the veteran all over, but a tough and hardy veteran. And no one who did not know his age would have set him down as less than two or three and forty, though as a matter of fact, he was only eight and thirty.

When I saw him put his great arms up and saw Tom Sayers advance towards him, I wondered how on earth the little "un" was going to get at him. But Tom looked equal to anything that was possible to man. Johnnie Gideon assured me that Sayers did not weigh an ounce more than 10st 8lb, so that he was giving away 50lbs in weight, and nearly 5 in, in height. Yet Tom was cheerful and his condition was superb. He was neat and clean made from head to heel. No great display of muscle in any particular place, but the strength evenly distributed everywhere- in the fine broad shoulders, the compact loins, the well-turned arms, the sinewy legs… Still, admirable specimen of an active and able- bodied athlete as he was, how was Tom going to get at the huge man- mountain with the arms like Maypoles? – That was the question. For the Slasher had made no secret of what his tactics would be. He was going to wait for the little "un", and depend on his powers as a counter-hitter to stall off and baffle all his attacks. I heard him make that statement over and over again, and I admired the good sense of his resolve. If he only kept to it!

But imagine the surprise of those who knew what the Slasher's avowed intention was, at seeing him pursue a course diametrically opposite to that he had so wisely laid down beforehand! Whether the sight of his diminutive foe roused his scorn, and the thought of Tom's cheek excited his indignation, but, instead of waiting the solid contempt and confidence we had expected for the onset of his foe. The Slasher his mind set to work at once.

The Slasher's terrific slogs were wasted. There must have been something wrong about the Tipton's eyesight for he misjudged his distance when letting go at Sayers when the blows would not have reached him. Tom did not stand still. He led the old Slasher a merry dance around the ring, till puffing and winded, the old "un" pulled up short and said "Coom and foight me, and don't prance loike a bloody dancing master".

But Tom only laughed; the Slasher would not learn wisdom from experience he felt certain that one blow from his mighty fist would un-sense Sayers. The Slasher stopped some of Tom's straight and swift deliveries. This was in the second round when after stopping Tom's left the Slasher in an exchange of counters, landed his right fair and square on Sayers's forehead and down went the little "un" like a floored skittle pin. Men who had never seen a fight before thought that this tremendous hit must have knocked Sayers senseless. But to their amazement when "Time" was called Tom came up to scratch, smiling, good tempered, and confident, and beyond a big lump on his forehead he seemed none the worst for a blow which looked hard enough to stave in the frontal bone of an ox. The round had lasted an hour and a half (it was the longest in the fight), and when the Slasher came up for number three he appeared greatly pleased with himself, and displayed his toothless jaw in a ghastly grin.

Blood Begins to Pour

But Tom was not going to let the big "un" get in any more flurries. His hitting was beautifully straight and clean. He cut the Slasher's right cheek open, bringing the blood out in a stream, and though the big "un" planted one or two smart ones on the neck and the side of the head, there was nothing like his full force behind the blows, and Tom didn't seem to mind them a bit. Indeed, his coolness was wonderful. He appeared already to have completely taken the measures of his Herculean adversary, and knew to an inch how near it was to go to him. Feinting, dodging, watch for an opening, like a cat for a mouse, Sayers kept the champion forever on the move, then suddenly darted in and landed a nasty one on the "mark". The Slasher followed him all over the ring, hitting out wildly with no manner of judgment, and, of course only tiring by these repeated misses. At last, finding that he could do nothing, the Tipton halted, put down his hands, and returned to his corner for another wipe from Jack MacDonald's sponge. Then, stretching his great muscular arms, and giving a knowing kind of shake of the head, as much to say, "Now I'm going to smash up this impudent little bantam". The Slasher bore down upon Tom, who was calmly waiting for him. There was some pretty stopping on the sides, for the Champion was a little more cautious now. Then Sayers got home cleverly on the side of the head. The Slasher looked very grim, but kept his temper and stopped Tom's next two attempts, well intended though they where, and got his right half-round on the little "un's" neck. Instantly Tom drove his left on the giant's nose, which seemed to go flat with a squelch, and the blood poured from both nostrils. This was more than the Slasher could stand. He rushed fiercely at his foe; Tom dodges quickly and cleverly, then saw his chance, and sent his right (the auctioneer) with tremendous force on the damaged cheek enlarging the grisly gash there. The blood bathed the Slasher's face and dripped on to his body. He paused for a moment, then turned around and walked to his corner to be sponged. I must say I never saw any man better seconded in the ring than William Perry up, almost as fresh as paint, after Tom's fist had drenched him in gore, was a thing that filled me with wonder and admiration.

Slasher now went to his man. There was something absolutely ferocious in his look. He would have killed Tom if he could have got a fair hold on him. But he was no match for Sayers in activity, and he utterly failed to bring his slippery enemy to book. The Champion's backers yelled to Sayers to stand still and let the Slasher get him. "No thankee", said Tom with a grin. His orders were to keep his man on his legs and fight him at long range and these orders he carried out to the letter. In vain the Slasher lashed out;

41. Jack MacDonald

129

every blow either missed or was stopped. His temper got the better of him. He rushed at Sayers, dashed out his right, and very narrowly escaped, smashing his fist against one of the stakes – his knuckles shaved the post. Sayers lifted up his arms in astonishment, and stood laughing, until the Slasher moved round on another tack and came at him again, when Tom slipped away, shaking his noddle and grinning. The big "un" blowing and puffing, followed, lunged out, missed and was promptly nailed on the nose by Tom's left.

Bang went the Slasher's right again- another miss – and this time Sayers gave him a smasher on the nose which turned on the claret-tap again. The infuriated Slasher rushed on, his nimble enemy danced round him slipped in when he saw an opening, dealt the Tipton another smasher on the nose, and was away before the ponderous fist of the Slasher was half - way on its journey to his head. Savage and puzzled, the Slasher stopped to consider, looked for a moment in a dazed sort of way at the exasperating little Jack-in-the-Box that defied all his efforts to crush

42. Bang on the Slasher's Boko

him, then with a snort which sent the blood flying from his nostrils, hurled himself on his foe. For once Tom was not quite quick enough. The blow grazed the side of his head, and down the little man went.

The first three rounds had occupied fifty-two minutes, and the Slasher was evidently fatigued by his exertions, but he was still confident of victory. Tom coolly and persistently played the game he had set before himself. He lured the great Colossus on to chase him round and round the ring, then, when the Slasher pulled up, puffing, panting, perspiring his nimble, fresh, and artful foe instantly wheeled round and went for him, sending his lightening expresses straight as a dart into the old warrior's face with stinging and cutting effect. But though the blood was from half a dozen wounds, the Slasher didn't seem to mind the blows; he would step back to his corner for a moment to have his face wiped with the wet sponge, and then pursue his fleet-footed foe in the same dogged, fruitless manner as before. He appeared wholly blind to the fact that he was stupidly throwing his strength away, and simply playing into the hands of his crafty antagonist.

As the fight went on, and the Slasher got more and more tired, the punishment Tom administrated was sickening to behold. Those bony fists of Sayers' worked awful havoc with the Tipton's feature. The thud with which the blows went home on that bruised and battered phiz made one involuntary cry "whew!" Another ripping slash sliced and mangled the upper lip, and before long both lips were hanging like great bleeding lumps of blubber over the disfigured and shapeless mouth. Another terrible right hander on the side of his face made the big "un's" jaw bulge out like a baboon's. A third laid open his right cheek, and the gash was trebled in size by repeated visitations on the sore spot. The man's whole face was covered with livid bruises till it looked like a rotten-ripe plum. And I felt positively sick when a slashing crack from Tom's right - the deadly "auctioneer" – cut through those pulpy lips like a knife through wet blotting-paper, and revealed the bleeding gums with the jagged stumps behind.

Time Called

With sight and senses nearly gone, a horrible, ghastly gory spectacle, this poor old Slasher fought on with the courage of despair, for his defeat meant not only disgrace but utter ruin to him. But his heroic struggle against failing nature was in vain, and it was a relief to everyone when in the ninth round, the end came in sight, and after another dreadful blow on the lacerated lips, followed by a regular doubler up on the mark, the Slasher reeled like a drunken ox, and fell as cattle ran. Surely this, everyone thought, must be the finish. But it wasn't, the Slasher doggedly refused to give in, and when "time" was called staggered towards the scratch. Such an awful object did he look with his gashed cheek, lacerated lips, and bulging jaw, that there were loud cries of "Take him away"; "he's beaten!". "Send him home!" "Don't let him fight any more!" "Don't you touch him, Tom; he's licked!"

Sayers stood in the centre of the ring with his arms folded and shrugged his shoulders, as much as to say "What am I to do if he doesn't know when he is beaten?" But he was spared the revolting task of inflicting more punishment on a man who was now utterly at his mercy. For Owen Swift stepped forward, held up his hands, and called to Sayers not to hit, as he should not allow the Slasher to fight any more.

43. The End

So, after a fight of one hour and forty-two minutes, with scarcely a mark on him, except a lump on his forehead and a slightly cut and swollen mouth, Tom Sayers won the Championship of England.

How could such a small man like Sayers do this to a great heavyweight? He could punch heavier than an average heavyweight. He had small hands with large knife- edged knuckles and they cut his opponent like knuckle dusters when they landed. He had perfected a slicing right arm blow which made full us of this. He was ten years younger than Bill Perry and approaching his peak. Bill was ten years past his.

Sayers had learned the hard way when he was defeated by Nat Langham that "a blinded opponent was a defeated opponent". He concentrated on his eyes, and so defeated Bill Perry, Tom Paddock and John Henan.

The opinion of most of the sporting personalities present was that Tom had deliberately set out to blind Perry, and the Tipton had not had fair play.

But so popular was he that the Corinthians had a collection for him sufficient to set him up once again in a Black Country beer house. This did not last long, for he was said to be incapable of business. His intelligence dulled and his physique ruined, he gradually went back to the canal boats and at one time was a night soil and stable manure contractor- taking boat loads between Tipton and Muckley Corner.

44. Whip-round

The Dudley Devil's prophecy came true over the years.

"Slasher, yoh'll stop as yoh started".

He had started on the night soil boat as a child and he returned to it as an old man. Any man over fifty years was old in those days.

"Yoh'll get all yoh gi'ed in one goo".

Before this fight with Tom Sayers he was virtually un-marked after twenty-one years in the Prize Ring. He had severely beaten Tass Parker, "Paddy" Dogherty, Ben Spilsbury and Jem Scunner among others and they carried his trade mark. If he did not get back from Sayers all that he had dished out to others he certainly got a proportion of it.

"Yoh and your pub will be parted".

Perry lost his pub, "The Champion of England", when he lost the fight.

133

"Tom Little will mek it cum true".

Tom Little or Little Tom Sayers did make it come true. Although his fighting physique had gone, his iron constitution remained and hard manual work and heavy drinking appeared not to affect him.

He was a good husband and good father- if he had lost a fortune, he worked hard until just before his end, and his family never knew the poverty to which the Black Country labourer was accustomed. "Big Will had shoulder blades like a pair of puddlers shovels" and his coffin was specially constructed to accommodate the breadth of his shoulders. "Will never laid a hand on his missus and children, and in drink was goodness itself, and don't forget a drunken brain speaks a sober mind. So long as he could work hard, have a quart, and sing "My Pretty Jane" he was happy. He loved children and the little lads used to spar with him. "Tell 'em, when yo grow up". He would say, "Yo've been in the ring with the Slasher, and 'it 'im on the nose".

In Perry's last fight, as in his early encounter with Jem Scunner just twenty years before, his old Black Country colleague and opponent, Tass Parker, was there in his corner. At the end there was nothing for it but to return to Tipton, to bask in the fame of having been the champion and to join an admiring visitor in a glass of spirits across his bar. He lived on, unlike most champions in this most physically punishing of sports, to past his sixtieth birthday. He was born when pugilism was still within easy reach of its best days. By the time he died, in 1880, it was within sight of its new beginnings with legalized boxing. It was not his fault, only his misfortune, to have been part of the sport at time when dubious commerce had replaced honest speculation, when winning was at a premium over fairness and none but the hardest bitten could survive for long.

Highgate Cemetery – The Resting Place Of Tom Sayers

In the early decades of the nineteenth century cemeteries faced a crisis. Inadequate burial space along with high mortality rates resulted in a lack of room for the dead. Graveyards and burial grounds were created between shops, houses and taverns - anywhere there was space. On occasions, undertakers dressed as clergy and

134

performed unauthorized and illegal funerals. Bodies were wrapped in cheap material and buried amongst other human remains in graves sometimes just a few feet deep. Quicklime was thrown over the body to help decomposition, so that within a few months the grave could be used again. The stench from these disease-ridden burial places was terrible. They were overcrowded, uncared for and neglected.

As successes go the Cemetery at Highgate was a great one, attracting a varied clientele and soon becoming one of the capital's most fashionable cemeteries.

"He Sin 'Em All Off"

Many sportsmen are buried here but in the pugilistic art of boxing it will come as no surprise to see the name SAYERS Thomas (1826-1865). His presence and his story are well-known. He went on to claim the Heavyweight title of England in 1857 controversially defeating the Slasher. The year after Sayers's retirement, the "Anti-prize Fight Act of 1861" was passed, which criminalised anyone who even

45. Thomas Sayers Grave

conveyed a member of the public to a fight. The Act virtually eliminated bare-knuckle fighting in England.

His burial was attended by ten thousand people. His friends again subscribed for the erection of a large tomb, bearing a statue of his beloved bull-mastiff.

You will see here a photograph I took of his grave in 1993 - the same year that the statue was unveiled to the Slasher. Sadly like most graves it had become overgrown and forgotten.

135

Fortunately there are the Friends of Highgate Cemetery and the St John's Preservation Group who work tirelessly to preserve their parks for the benefit of grave owners and visitors.

The Last Fight

The 1871 census gives Bill's occupation as a Contractor Boatman. Bill gained a livelihood on the canal by selling night soil to farmers of Codsall and Albrighton. On one of these outings the Slasher's boat nearing Aldridge with Perry steering and his son employed by him driving the horse on the old towpath, he came into confrontation with a Shropshire Union Fly Boat. It is a recognized rule that one gave way to these boats, the Slasher through a spirit of perverseness kept going, resulting in the jamming of the Bridge Hole by the two boats. One can easily imagine the selective language used between the four men on the fly boat and old Tipton. Bill would not have been easily ruffled by their dire threats. "Hold on" said Bill "I'll come to thee" and jumped on to the fly boat. No sooner had he landed when one young lad rushed at him only to be met with a fearful Sock Dollager full in the middle of the face, sending him a clear twenty-feet into the canal. His mate came on the scene and proceeded to help on to dry land and on doing so a man who witnessed the whole affair shouted "You darn fools doe yoh now who he is, it's the Tipton Slasher". There was no more show of fighting by the four fly boat men who proceeded to liberate their boat and continue their journey along the cut.

Records give the fight as being in the year 1876, Slasher would have been 57 years of age. Not bad for an ode'un.

This newer mode of men's minds must not be forgotten when reviewing Perry's neglected later years. He was no longer the "Slasher". His old activity had forsaken him, his eyesight began to fail him, and the remnant of his saving was fast dwindling away before he had fully realized pugilism would no longer avail him as a means of likelihood. About this period it is related of him that he one day entered the smoke room of a favourite public house in Tipton dressed in a smock frock, and a slouch hat, when a gentleman present, a prominent member of the Local Board, offered to treat him. A flash of pride for those bygone days when he had associated with the rich and the influential came to Perry's eye, and as he whipped out of his pocket a roll of bank notes he ungraciously replied that he could pay for his own drinks.

A SECOND OPINION – MY OWN VIEW

The Slasher after his fight with Sayers was described as a broken man, forgotten by his friends and physically damaged. But was he so physically and mentally inept? Research begs to differ. Tom Langley described him in his broadcast in an evocative and heart rending way. As to his health, if he was so seriously injured why did he appear in a joint benefit with Tom Sayers?

"Joint benefit of Tom Sayers and the Tipton Slasher

A benefit for the present and Ex-Champion has been announced and will take place on Monday week at the Clandos Street Rooms, when they will be assisted by the elite of the fancy and who as a windup will fight their battle again.

Who can doubt it will be a bumper."

This benefit was held one week after the fight, so was the Slasher physically damaged as reported in the papers."

The Slasher had backed himself as always with every farthing he had. Backing himself at odds of 6/4 selling his cups, medals, rings and trophies, even his own beer house, the Champion of England, Spon Lane, West Bromwich. A beer house was described as a low house, this was Slasher's life, a life that he ruled and enjoyed. It was to be his last performance in the Prize Ring and he was determined that it should not be unworthy of his well earned fame. The fight ended in disaster for the Slasher, everything he owned had been lost, his beer house was sold as soon as the Articles were signed. The

Slasher was described as done for, utterly ruined. Tom Sayers along with the Corinthians collected a respectable amount, while another collection enables him to take another beer house in Tipton. It is stated that he lost the beer house after a few months as he had no head for business. Old Tipton took stock after the fight and following his benefit with Tom Sayers, realized money was still to be made at benefits for himself. His canvas stall was a popular site at race courses and wakes, selling pies and refreshments. The Slasher was still drinking and gambling heavy, he even lost one of his boxing booths in a card game. He was known to offer a guinea to any man who could stay with him in the ring for five minutes. Such was his challenge, he attracted many a tough miner and chain maker who were anxious to gain a reputation as having fought the ex Champion of England. He did have an eye for business and making money and in 1861 took over the Brick Layers Arms Wolverhampton, 4 years after his defeat by Sayers. The census shows the inhabitants as being Will, his wife Ann Maria, son William and domestic servant Mary Walker. The beer house was attended by the local sporting fraternity. Beer Houses were the resort of dog fighters, pigeon flyers, cock fighters and pugilists to say nothing of old time bull baiters. More than one tap room in Tipton has been cleared at the request of a fearless customer who desired to try conclusions with the Slasher. Many a friendly bout has ended in the retirement from the ring, not by the Slasher but the customer.

The Last Years

The Slasher had moved to Bilston. In 1880 the year of his death, he was described as a General Dealer of Scrap Iron, still making a penny in the latter years. He owned his house, not huge but comfortable, a mean feat in those days, so was the Slasher inept? I do not think so, a lover of life? Yes. A gambler? Yes but still a provider for his family. He was described as a good husband and father. He had lost a fortune but worked hard until just before his end.

Title Benefits

The Pugilistic Benefit in Aid of the Patriotic Fund

Benefits had two aims; one was to help boxers who had fallen on hard times, secondly to reward both winner and loser of previous encounters.

William was known to appear at many benefits for fellow old and injured boxers. Easy pickings were to be made from tours and exhibitions. The Slasher went on a provincial tour before his fight with Harry Broom. The one offer of a sparring and fighting tour through the United States was turned down, reason cited as "Sea Sickness". There appears to be a big difference between the cut at Tipton and the Atlantic Ocean.

Tom Langley's Broadcast

Tom Langley's book "The Tipton Slasher His Life and Times" is regarded as the Bible to the Slasher, a detailed account written by him. But a new transcript has come to life regarding the great man and features a story regarding Charles Freeman which shows the strange and dubious betting of the Slasher and his followers. Tom's opinion cannot be ignored.

Monday 23rd January 1962.

"This is the Midland Home Service. "The Tipton Slasher".

In 1819 William Perry was born in Park Lane, Tipton and is probably the only Tipton man to become world famous. As a prize fighter he was for many years Champion of England, and this evening Tom Langley is to recall some of the exciting moments in the life and times of the Tipton Slasher."

The above and description opposite are taken from the original script read by Tom Langley.

"The Slasher before he was 20 was fighting for big money, always winner takes all, he feared no one, but most fighters feared him. There was one defeat recorded against the Slasher which requires an explanation. Ben Caunt had an eye on the economic value of the entertainment stage, and on his return from the USA, he brought with him Charles Freeman, a seven foot freak who was not a fighter. A match was made between this fearsome fellow and the fearless Slasher. It captured the imagination of the fancy and it is said that all the available money in Tipton was placed on the Yankee and the Birmingham bookmakers couldn't understand it, but the Tiptonians had heard a whisper. There is no doubt that in this fight the Slasher had been paid not to hurt him.

Those who would not have exchanged the time of day with him, had he been a boatman, sought his company, he had no time for them. Unfortunately for him they were mostly literate members of the Tipton hierarchy and it was from then the story spread that he was a dour, ignorant, unsmiling brute of a man. Those that knew him best, my grandfather amongst them, left a different picture of him. A rough tongued typical Black Country man, as kindly as his expression. Outside the ring a kindly man with a good singing voice, he liked everybody to know who he was. If a man got awkward in his pub, he just lifted him up and put him out into Spon Lane. The Slasher after his fight with Sayers was a terrible sight, he never breathed through his nose again.

He was deaf in one ear and his eyesight had gone. He peered about him like a lost soul, nobody wanted to know him accept a few old pals.

There shall never be another fighter like him. He could have eaten Jack Johnson and Jim Jeffreys before breakfast. John L Sullivan would have been a bladder of lard to him."

Closing Announcement

"In that recorded talk the speaker was Tom Langley."

CHAMPION OF ENGLAND
1850 - 1857

He was the Champion of England at Bare Knuckle Fighting
From Tipton he came an he was faster than lightening
William Perry was is nairm
An Boxin' was his gairm

Son of a Miner an he cudn't arf box
Heart of a Lion and strong as an Ox
The Tipton Slasher he was to becum

Cummin from Tipton cuzz that was his um
The Fountain was his Boozer where he learnt to train
He held on to the title for a seven 'ear reign
Born in 1819 and at 61 he did die

The flewer wor the plairce that he liked to lie
The Great mon himself now stonds in his classic stance
Imagine yerself cumin up against this Bull of a Mon
He'd bost all ya fairce and half ya teeth ud be gone

If he was as hard as the Bronze he is Med
I'm glad he's a statue and glad he's still jed.

By Peter Hill
2009

The Final Words Taken From The Childhood Scrapbook.

The beginnings of prize-fighting or boxing for money with bare fists lived on brutality but died of boredom after the Slasher's demise. The old Prize Ring was brutal compared to the gloved encounters that followed.

At one time he was the darling of the aristocracy who followed the fight game and gold was no stranger to his pocket.

He saw Tom Sayers, Paddock, the two Broomes and many others pass onto their graves. This is the closing scene of the Tipton's long and chequered career, he had punched his way to fame.

But then that is the lesson life teaches to those with eyes to see. No-one is above price - be it money, fame or power.

"It Ay Natural"

Tipton Phrases of Humour from the Ode Tipton Spark

- Man retreating from a fight said "It's better to be a coward for a day then a dead bloke all your life".

- The next best boxer to the Slasher was AA Walters the local undertaker. It was said that when he put them down they day get back up again.

- I aye never bin any good but I'm a damn sight better than yoe.

- Doe trust a bloke that has a puss, a ponytail and doe drink.

- The Romans never conquered Tipton, so great was their fear of the Tipton Tatters stealing their horses, chariots and bronze armour, they gave it a wide berth.

- The God-fearing Vikings failed to invade Tipton as the cuts were not yet dug.

- It's a hard life being a cabbage but tougher if you're a Brussels sprout.

142

- Last time I set eyes on you, you were out of sight already.

- It aye stopped raining since it started.

- This body was once a temple now it's a ruin.

- The first crossword was published by Tipton's Horace Webb in 1836. Horace is buried in Tipton Cemetery. You go through the old gates and you will find his grave - four down two across.

Appendix 1

Contributors to the First Appeal

Mr Hugh Corbett. Dudley	5s
Mr Ben Tranter. Dudley	5s
Mr Luke Walters. Dudley	5s
Mr David Jones. Dudley	5s
Mr Cliff Ritson. Dudley	5s
Mr Dick Henshaw. Dudley	5s
Mr Walter Marsh. Dudley	5s
Mr E Crowe. Dudley	5s
Mr Edwin Perry. Stockton on Tees	5s
Anon (per Rev. D. H. S. Mould)	5s
Mr Harold Press	5s
Mr Harry Jones. Dudley	5s

Further Contributors

Previously acknowledged	£18.11s 0
Mr J. B. Bradley. Dudley	5s
Mr J. Hanbury. Australia	5s
Mr J. Hanbury. Bolton	5s
Liverpool Stadium Seconds	5s
Mr Jack Hanlon. Liverpool	5s
Mr J. A. Shepherd. Sedgley	5s

Appendix 2

Illustrations and Photographs

Appendix 3

Acknowledgments & Bibliography

Pugilistica. The early history of British boxing containing lives of the most celebrated pugilists by Henry Downes Miles

Boxiana. A series of volumes of boxing articles written by early 19th century English sportswriter/journalist Pierce Egan

Bell's Life in London and Sporting Chronicle. A British weekly sporting paper published as a pink broadsheet between 1822 and 1886.

The Tipton Slasher: His Life and Times by Tom Langley

David Christie Murray 1847-1907 journalist and writer of many novels

F W Hackwood - historian and author

Fights for the Championship by Francis L. Dowling

Express and Star. An evening newspaper based in Wolverhampton, published Monday to Saturday in nine different editions covering the Black Country, Birmingham and the wider West Midlands area from Tamworth to Kidderminster

Black Country Bugle. A nostalgic newspaper which serves the Black Country region and has been in circulation since April 1972. The paper is published weekly by Staffordshire Newspapers. The paper has an office located at Bugle House, 41 High Street, Cradley Heath

Keith Hodgkins - for his help and local knowledge

John & Sue Oakley - there from the start

Pete Hill - Ale taister and poet

Helena - for all her help

Life & Times by Philopugilis

Championship sketches with portraits by Alfred Holt

Fistiana, by the editor of Bells Life in London

Boxing a chronology of the Ring

Fisticuffs & personalities of the Prize Ring

Boxers and their battles by Thormanby

Fights Forgotton by Henry Sayers

Fights for the Championship

Famous Fights Police Budget edition

The Prize Ring

Brewers Of Genuine Beers Since 1877

www.bathams.co.uk

First Class Financial Management Limited

Sound Local Adviser Shows How Experience & Reliability

Can give professional financial protection to you and your family

"Yo cor beat FCFML for bostin independent advice"

8, St Michael's Court

Victoria Street

West Bromwich

B70 8ET

0121 553 0707 (T)

0121 525 0580 (F)

ron@newman1066.fsnet.co.uk

First Class Financial Management Limited is an appointed representative of Sesame Ltd
which is authorised and regulated by the Financial Services Authority

MILLICHIPS SOLICITORS

Millichips are a well established Firm of Solicitors in West Bromwich, having been practising in the Black Country since the 1870's.

The origin of Millichips practising in West Bromwich dates back to the 1870's. Until the 1930's the firm was known as Sharpe & Darby. At that time the original 'Millichip', A A Millichip, became a partner, and following the death of the Mr Darby, the firm became known as Sharpe & Millichip.

A A Millichip was succeeded by his nephew Bert Millichip (subsequently Sir Bert Millichip). Sir Bert carried on the practice in West Bromwich as a sole practitioner until the 1970's when the firm grew to become a six partner firm.

In 1990 Sharpe & Millichip merged with Tyndallwoods to become Tyndallwoods & Millichip. At that time the firm had five offices in West Bromwich, Edgbaston, Corporation Street, Chinatown and Saltley. In 1994 a demerger took place and the firm of Millichips emerged, retaining offices in Edgbaston and West Bromwich. 1996 saw a restructuring of the partnership to its present day form with the original West Bromwich in High Street office and a new office in Solihull.

Our Office in West Bromwich provides a complete legal service and has the following specialist departments: Commercial Conveyancing, Business Sales and Purchases, Residential Conveyancing, Family and Child Care, Personal Injury and Clinical Negligence, Wills, Trusts and Probate, General Civil & Commercial Litigation and the resolution of disputes.

We also have a further office in Solihull which specialises in Commercial Conveyancing, Business Sales and Purchases, Residential Conveyancing, Employee Relocation Work, Wills, Trusts and Probate.

Our staff are friendly, approachable, discreet and expert in their specialised areas.

Offices

317-319 HIGH STREET, WEST BROMWICH B70 8LU
TEL: 0121 500 6363 FAX: 0121 553 1519

4 THE COURTYARD, WARWICK ROAD, SOLIHULL B91 3DA
TEL: 0121 624 4000 FAX: 0121 624 8400

Regulated by the Solicitors Regulation Authority No. 78530

BATES & DAVIS
Transfer Station

* Self deliveries welcome
* Open to the public
* Skips in all sizes, Midi to Roll on Bodies
* Best Rates Around

☎ *Call us <u>First</u> on...*

0121 557 3346 or 07956 375 157
Ask for Allan

152